D1258602

Art in Service of the Sacred

Catherine Kapikian
edited by Kathy Black

Abingdon Press
Nashville

ART IN SERVICE OF THE SACRED

This book is printed on recycled, acid-free paper.

Library of Congress Cataloging-in-Publication Data

Kapikian, Catherine A. (Catherine Andrews), 1939-
    Art in service of the sacred / Catherine Kapikian ; Kathy Black, editor.
    p. cm.
    ISBN 0-687-35863-9
    1. Christianity and art. 2. Liturgy and art. 3. Church decoration and ornament. I. Black, Kathy, 1956- II. Title.

    N7830.K28 2006
    246—dc22

                 2005033952

06 07 08 09 10 11 12 13 14 15—10 09 08 07 06 05 04 03 02 01

MANUFACTURED IN THE UNITED STATES OF AMERICA

Art in Service of the Sacred comes at the most opportune time for those interested in the visual arts and Christian faith. With a reawakening to the visual in the life of the church, this book will prove to be a most valuable source, both for its insight into the critically important role of the visual arts and also for its practical suggestion. It is a must for all artists dedicated to the revival of art in the church.

> Sandra Bowden
> President, Christians in the Visual Arts (CIVA)

This exposition of the artist/church relationship in designing and creating liturgical art is achieved only through Kapikian's decades of toil and determination. She provides insightful examples of how revelatory the process can be. This should be required reading for both artists and church leaders.

> Tyrus R. Clutter
> Director, Christians in the Visual Arts (CIVA)

Ms. Kapikian's *Art in Service of the Sacred* captures in word and thought what her art exquisitely expresses in sanctuaries across the nation-a deep appreciation of the relationship between beauty and worship, space and spirituality, universal symbol, and site-specific interpretation. She makes an important contribution to worship design in the 21st century.

> Dr. Robert W. Henderson
> Sr. Pastor, Westminster Presbyterian Church, Greensboro, NC

Art in Service of the Sacred is a rich resource for bringing the vitality of the arts, especially the visual arts, into congregations in a dynamic way that integrates them into worship, education, community, and outreach. With a rare blend of vigour and delicacy, Catherine Kapikian conveys the intimacy of creativity and spirituality and its capacity for nurturing healthy life in the church and our world.

> Laurel Gasque
> Religious & Theological Studies Fellowship of Canada

Kapikian performs a valuable and much-needed service to communities of faith by showing us how art helps us to encounter the sacred and opens the way to experiences of transformation beyond the realm of words.

> Frank T. Griswold
> Presiding Bishop of the Episcopal Church

At last! Here is a book about the work of Catherine Kapikian, the visionary pioneer of art and theology. Like a liturgical arts' Christo, she has engaged and enlivened whole religious communities in the creation of sacred spaces for many years. *Art in Service of the Sacred* shows Kapikian's aesthetic at work in her powerful art. Now the brilliant thinking, solid and passionate, behind her work is shared with the reader. Those who know and love Catherine Kapikian recognize her voice: at once witty and sharp, yet full of humility and poetic truth-telling.

Kathy T. Hettinga
Distinguished Professor of Art, Messiah College
Design Director, Christians in the Visual Arts (CIVA)

Catherine Kapikian's artistic creations exude biblical and symbolic content, celebrating historic and mythic events. Abstractly, effectively, she transmits awe and wonder of the Holy, of mystery and revelation, with necessary spiritual ambiguity. Such ambiguity woos the imagination of her viewers, and nourishes those who "see in a mirror dimly," who "know in part," and who seek spiritual understanding.

Eli Takesian
Former Chief of Chaplains, U. S. Marine Corps

Art in Service of the Sacred affirms that the relationship between art and the Church is extraordinarily close. The Church fulfills the aesthetic, and art embodies the transcendent. Kapikian's book also shows that this relationship must be negotiated by each artist in their own particular way. This is Kapikian's way.

Daniel A. Siedell
Curator, Sheldon Memorial Art Gallery,
University of Nebraska-Lincoln

Artist Catherine Kapikian is a tireless advocate for the arts in the seminary and the congregation. This book is a gallery of valuable, practical essays that must be read by artists, committees, and clergy before engaging in the creation of art for liturgical environments.

Richard S. Vosko, Ph.D., Hon. AIA
Liturgical Design Consultant

For Kathy Black,
insistent and thoughtful.
As midwife and manna,
you fit and fed my effort.

Contents

FOREWORD: Experiencing the Sacred   9

PROLOGUE: Calling to Worship   13

ONE: Welcoming the Artist   15

TWO: Mediating the Word   31

THREE: Reading Liturgical Space   43

FOUR: Transforming Space   51

FIVE: Reclaiming Symbols   65

SIX: Evoking the Creative Process   89

SEVEN: Engaging in Participatory Aesthetics   107

EIGHT: Sponsoring Artists-in-Residence   119

NINE: Integrating Art and Theology   135

TEN: Integrating Art and Theology
    in Context: DVD Images   147

EPILOGUE: Sending Forth   171

APPENDIX: Outline of DVD Chapters   172

Experiencing the Sacred

*A*s a pastor and professor of worship, I have been deeply interested in the role the various arts play in creating sacred space, in evoking the participation of the entire congregation, and in providing avenues for each of us to experience the Holy One among us; to encounter God.

While almost all worship includes a variety of art forms such as music, poetry, and rhetoric, many congregations today are experimenting with using drama, dance, and a multiplicity of visual forms as well. Various artistic mediums have been used throughout the history of worship including statuary, tapestries, paintings, mosaics, stained glass windows, and architecture. The Protestant reformers wanted to simplify the worship environment so the laity could focus on the hearing of God's word rather than on the visual stimuli surrounding them. Consequently, preaching became paramount, and our worship spaces became devoid of the symbols, beauty, and spiritual meaning that art can evoke. Many Protestants have recognized the importance of aesthetics within the liturgical environment to create sacred space and are reclaiming the role of art in worship and congregational life. The use of the arts in worship helps the congregation to integrate their senses with their intellect, the verbal Word and visual or kinesthetic expressions of that Word.

There are other congregations, however, that are trying to be sensitive to the unchurched, to the seekers in our society. In an attempt to make seekers more comfortable, these churches are removing religious art and symbol from the worship space. They believe that the architecture of corporate office buildings and warehouses is more accessible to the unchurched. Therefore, creating a "contemporary" or "corporate" feel within the worship space is more important than creating "sacred space" for this population. These congregations are removing crosses, banners, paraments, and vestments in an effort to create an inoffensive environment for these seekers, particularly those in the Baby Boom generation.

The liturgical reform movement has recognized the importance of sacred space, symbol, and art in worship for decades. But even churches like Willow Creek and those within the "Emerging Church" movement who are targeting the younger, Millennial generation are recognizing that the aesthetics within the liturgical environment and the use of relevant symbols are important elements in providing an atmosphere where people can experience the mystery and the presence of God.[1]

Historically, church architecture and art proclaimed a transcendent God who was inaccessible to the people. But in the last several decades, many churches have emphasized the immanence of God to such a degree that we have lost sight of the fact that we cannot fully comprehend the totality of God's nature. We have lost the sense of mystery, awe, and wonder.

We recognize that in many congregations, large screens, microphones, and amplifiers (symbols of modern society) have taken a predominant visual role in worship and have replaced the traditional religious symbols of cross, candles, altar, and font. With society's increasing dependence on technology, this may continue well into the future. These congregations often project visual images on the screen as backdrop or illustration throughout the service. Some congregations use projected images of paintings or other forms of art on the screen. Others use film clips or are creating digital art to be used in worship.

This book encourages congregations to take seriously the role of *visual art* in worship and in the broader life of the church. It proclaims the power of art when it is used as art (not merely back-

---

1. The "Emerging Church" movement is targeting those who are seeking a sense of mystery and is attracting a number of 18–25 year-olds. Candles and crosses and creating sacred space through various art forms are crucial components in their worship services. See *Emerging Worship* by Dan Kimball.

drop or illustration), reclaims the presence of religious symbols in worship, asserts the importance of the aesthetic dimensions of ecclesial space, and recovers the role of visual art to engage our senses and our imaginations as we seek to encounter the Holy One in our lives.

One of the unique and exciting aspects of this book is that it is written by a professor of art and religion who is also a renowned artist, Catherine Kapikian. The book is for the artist as well as the church, interpreting the church to the artist and the artist to the church. It highlights the importance of dialogue between the church and the artist so that each can challenge and inspire the other. For Christians the source of imagination and creativity is rooted in God who is Creator, and we understand ourselves to be made in the image of God. We are creatures who are called to create.

With a trained and playful imagination, Kapikian designs for congregations in the space that they inhabit for their communal worship of God. Too often clergy and parishioners know their worship space needs help. They know when they enter it that it does not evoke a sense of the sacred mystery of God. But their imaginations are not trained to see alternative possibilities. The artist is trained to "see" differently, to help us envision an expression of our beliefs and yearnings visually, in a particular space.

Kapikian's work spans the spectrum of very large designs (a 60' x 22' *Last Supper*) to much smaller creations, from permanent installations to temporary art that creates a worship environment for specific occasions. She also creates vestments and paraments that utilize the colors and symbols of the liturgical year while simultaneously mirroring the artistic installations within the liturgical space. Kapikian's work is multilayered, playing with color and symbol in such a way that it evokes a sense of awe and mystery. Her art transforms in ways that provide glimpses into the Divine and acknowledge that there is more to God than we can ever express. Her art draws people in, time after time, to find new meaning, new insight, new experiences with the Holy. The visual art works with the architecture to create a sense of sacred space where the presence of God can be felt.

While she has done the actual fabrication of her artwork, she also provides designs to congregations who then engage church members to create the art themselves, within community. Working in fabric, needlepoint yarn, wood, and/or paint, members of the congregation become co-creators as they enhance their communal space.

The DVD included with this book shows scores of photographs of her art: before and after photographs of sanctuary spaces that have been totally transformed, vestments and paraments for the various seasons within the liturgical year, and temporary liturgical art for conferences and retreat settings. There are also images depicting the transformation of a narthex, fellowship hall, balcony, and church hallway. Along the way, you will also be treated to Kapikian's creative process, from the original imaginings to the completed project.

In addition to her art, however, I believe that as an artist, Kapikian has much to say to the church and to other artists. So for the past few years, I have urged, prodded, even coerced this reluctant artist/scholar to offer her insights and wisdom to a broader audience through the medium of the printed text. Her writing is a blend of astute insight with poetic perspective. I believe it is a rich resource that explores the dynamics between art, artist, and the church. As you read through the book and view the various images, may you be inspired and challenged to rethink the ways art as product and process can transform space and community in service of the sacred. Blessings on the journey.

Kathy Black
Claremont, 2005

PROLOGUE:

Calling to Worship

$\mathcal{T}$he impulse to consider art, theology, and religious ritual together began early. Roller-skating or biking past my beloved Bethesda by the Sea Episcopal Church, I would drink in its reassuring presence while the memory of the minister's benediction, "The peace of God which passes all understanding...," caressed my soul.[2]

Stop, see, and be. That is what I did. Whether through a fleeting tryst in the formal gardens, a stolen peek through a side door, a contrived excursion to choir practice with my brothers, or a moment caught by the wonder of Sunday worship, my head and heart dwelt in this lofty and shimmering place. Bethesda by the Sea loomed large in contrast to the extravagant abundance of little flowers and lush landscape that anchored it. Inside, the radiance of sun-drenched colored glass coupled with the enormity of dazzling sound conspired in worship to conjure up within me a notion that God was real and resided in this place.

Drawing, painting, or building models from scratch, my self-understanding as artist emerged early. How proud I was of my stagecoach, its intricate turnings fashioned from flat strips of balsa wood, its shiny red sides and black spoked wheels the consequence of many sandings and reapplication of Testors paint. When I copied a picture of a princess three times its original size, in comparable format, my mother complimented me so extravagantly that it galvanized a way of thinking about shifting scales. Showered with supplies while simultaneously

---

2. Bethesda by the Sea Episcopal Church is located in Palm Beach, Florida.

buoyed by parental encouragement, my aptitude for transcending materials grew. So did my enthrallment. In time, God and place played out as a conviction that the Holy is ushered in through the mysterious alchemy of manipulated materials. Intricately tied to praise and awe, my attempts at creating art became stabs at making those remembered moments of childhood visible. This conviction wrought long ago keeps me in its clutch.

Alongside this reality rest two others, just as potent: one propels me to the studio, the other to worship. Obliquely caught within each of my constructions rest the reverberating markings by which I manage the din of daily coping. In the guise of veiled metaphors for living, my works chart turbulent territory. Through the reconfiguration of materials, I work through the joys and sorrows of living. The makings of my works are forged from creative processes that happen to tug and pull in the direction of belief. Because these processes resonate with the truth of the church's proclamations, they continually call me back to it.

Despite contemporary culture's bias for the autonomy of the artist and her art, I view the art-making enterprise as relational. My work is incomplete until it arrives and lives within the community that commissioned it. Born out of religious community, the work exists for the sake of spiritual community. All I know is that I must create it, all the while striving that it be more than mere illustration and propaganda. The judgment of its merits or lack thereof is someone else's task.

These attempts at making the unseen visible, marking my daily coping, and charting correspondences between my creative process and the church's proclamations comprise a working triad in which one aspect interpenetrates and enhances the others. This complexity not only issues forth in my works but also quickens, by analogy, my appreciation for the possibility of a God characterized by a Triune construction. Predictably, I and oftentimes some of my work land in worship.

CHAPTER ONE

Welcoming the Artist

Face to face I must confront my works,
*   bold colors, transparent meanderings,*
*   metaphors,*
*   created to capture and curtail.*
Now, a forced revisit.
Robbed of their contexts,
*   homeless,*
*   they vie for attention,*
*   in digital disarray.*
This effort takes courage.
Its process feels vexing.
Perhaps I will join myself,
*   an artist on the line.*

*T*hese works yield insights for others in contexts rich in shared meaning. They live in community, sometimes for a weekend, other times for several months of recycling each year, and oftentimes for years of permanent encounter. Some works no longer exist. That is how it should be. Each new generation must recreate its proclamations, embody the essence of its musings, secure its stabs at evocations of the Holy in material forms. Very occasionally, one will endure.

My works are site-specific; apart from their sites they make no sense. My works in ecclesial spaces attempt a visual completeness of the whole through clarity and unity of form with their surroundings.[3] They belong to the ritual moment. Such work is not decoration, an appendage like excessive, colorful frostings

---

3. Ecclesial: of or relating to a church.

15

on a cake or stripes on a pair of stockings. It is work designed to bring into focus why our structures are. Such work amplifies, intensifies the moment wherein we, in oneness, worship and know God. Separating my site-specific works from their contexts, making them available to a mass audience through digital technology, and offering them for inclusion in this book are alien to the impulse that generated them.

Sitting down to write raises the perennial question, "What is art?" In our postmodernist times, some say it is anyone's guess. And when is it good, and who says so? *The New York Times* devoted a full page to the answers, answers given by museum directors, art critics, artists, and art world observers.[4]

Many decades ago we possessed a different sense of what art is. Then the prevailing consensus posited that painting, sculpting, and drawing issued from creative processes grounded in traditions of passed-on skills and anchored to aesthetic principles. The consensus in dominant U.S. culture today states that anything can be called art, providing its maker intended it to be. Intentionality is the sole attribute of designation around which most members of the present-day art world concur and coalesce. Our present-day notion of what qualifies as art, while hugely broad, still leaves issues unaddressed. For instance, if a person's motivation and therefore intention is to create a work for function, is this person denied the designation of artist despite the aesthetic merit of his or her work? Our present-day notion of what stands as art, while hugely egalitarian, nevertheless precludes the designation of artist for hobbyists who create worthy works. The hobbyist does not think of and therefore intend his or her work as art. Yet works of some hobbyists give evidence of a conceptual leap of thought from their predecessors, a long held conviction in the art world designating the mark of an artist.

Several things can be said with certainty. Standards and criteria for judging the works of living artists vary. The artists who rise to national acclaim do so in a celebrity-worshiping, superstar-

---

4. *"Is It Art? Is It Good? And Who Says So?" The New York Times,* Sunday, Oct. 12, 1997.

saturated culture. How often an artist earns critical acclaim based on the merit of his or her work, rather than on a dedicated process of promotion, is a question worth asking. If confusion over these issues suggests that we simply throw up our hands, think again. Imagine a world without art.

Dare I attempt a definition wide enough to envelop the scope of works in our world? Art is the articulated metaphor of an engaged perception: the artist replaces an impulse, idea, and/or train of thought with a work bearing likeness.

Thus it happens that today a hole in the ground is art if its creator collaborates with the dirt, intentionally shaping an artistic configuration, and transports it (hole plus surrounding) to a context (maybe a gallery) where it is viewed as art. Some assert that art is in a state of demise, anarchy at least, while others posit the death of art, an interesting idea considering it coincides with a circulating notion that God is dead.

Each is very much alive. Both exhibit complex phenomena. While art connoisseurs grope with standards of accountability (and whose standards anyhow?), religious leaders grapple with methods of denominationally diverse proclamations. Together they face the ongoing battle of persuading seeker on behalf of her soul, or art connoisseur on behalf of his well-being that their proclamations and products are efficacious. It is not an accident that the parallel worlds of art and religion collide in common purpose. The two are siblings of the same bloodline. Both evoke meaning regarding matters of ultimacy through structures of doctrinal discourse or works of materials transcended.

> Theology and the arts are architectures of meaning, fragile structures through whose doors and windows we glimpse the mystery of our being. Hungry to hear and see some part of the truth about ourselves, we go to church, the synagogue, the theatre. Each time we hope to be called by name, to be surprised, reminded of who we are and whose we are.

The artist and the theologian share the task of
inviting us across these mysterious thresholds.[5]

Despite their natural affinity, too often they exist in isolation, a pity
for siblings and a tragedy for the human family. In our age of spe-
cialization of functions, they appear as noisy friends rather than
attentive siblings. In earlier times in the Christian West, we have
seen art as the handmaiden of religion. In this model's evolution,
we have witnessed a subservience that allows religion to reject or
recast the image, bending it to propagandistic conformity, didactic
function, and evangelistic purpose. This controlling grip upon the
artist by the church ensures works of banality and mediocrity. In
his long poem "The Minister," the Welsh priest and poet R.S.
Thomas wrote:

> Protestantism—the adroit castrator
> Of art; the bitter negation
> Of song and dance and the heart's
> innocent joy—
> You have botched our flesh and left us
> only the soul's
> Terrible impotence in a warm world.[6]

Today, broadly speaking, the artistic community and the religious community observe one another across a divide. Those
clergy in the church disinterested in pursuing a relationship set
forth some or all of the following reasons, reasons related to
themselves or related to what they think their congregation
thinks. These clergy insist upon the supremacy of words for setting forth truth claims, suspect that art's sensuality seduces people from a reasoned faith, reject art's presumed elitism, fear
idolatry of the image, posture a work ethic and moral stance
assumed superior to the artist's, tout lack of financial resources
for activity unrelated to social outreach, and lament their full
schedules which preclude extra commitments.

---

5. Judith Rock. Taken from a brochure of AURA (Association Uniting Religion and Art), an ecumenical group of artists and clergy in Philadelphia
   who commenced their work in 1985.
6. *Faith and the Arts: The Inaugural Lecture of the Arts and Crafts Guild*, given
   by Bishop Michael Marshall at Holy Trinity Church, London, England,
   September 22, 1998.

These issues belie the more compelling reasons for church leadership's widespread indifference to and lack of support for contemporary art. The root cause is ignorance of art history, particularly modern art history, art criticism, and art theory. Furthermore, the abstraction, if not outright obliteration, of recognizable subject matter by the bulk of today's artists in their image-making means there is no easy entry into their work. It is easier to engage with work that bears realistic resemblance to external appearances. Abstract and nonobjective works make access difficult for those who, despite lack of knowledge of these histories, desire to connect with what they see. Undergirding access and fundamental to it is a person's degree of fluency in the non-verbal vocabulary of the visual. Its language and syntax is alien for many.[7] Knowledge of this language is critical especially when looking at abstract and non-objective imagery. If theological proclamation couched in this language is incomprehensible, its support, therefore, is unsustainable. These facts demonstrate the need for—at the very least—rudimentary clergy education in the arts. Lastly, leadership is ignorant of the processes by which artists create their finished product, oftentimes leery of the artists' way of making thought visible.

Artists look across the divide and register their reasons too. Many are disinterested in the church while others cannot imagine the church as a context for their work. Those who do wish for acknowledgement from the church simultaneously suspect that support means loss of control over aesthetic choices, censorship by church clientele.

Granted, the mandates of the two communities are distinctive, but are they not complimentary? Who then is responsible for bridging the chasm? Pope Paul VI made an overture when he spoke to a group of Italian artists invited to the Sistine Chapel.

---

7. Non-verbal visual vocabulary is comprised of the elements of line, shape, value (the relative relationships of lights to darks), color with its three attributes (hue refers to red, yellow, blue, orange, green, purple or variations thereof); value (colors range from light like yellow to dark like purple); intensity (colors are bright like chartreuse and dull like pea green); and texture (either applied to a work or simulated to represent the surface quality of an object); syntax refers to the arrangement of the elements of non-verbal vocabulary used to create balance, movement, pattern, repetition, dominance, subordination, harmony, rhythm, and proportion.

I am not your friend so much by reason of patronage as for a more intrinsic reason, namely, that our ministry needs your collaboration. In our ministry we must preach, make understandable and accessible the world of the spirit, the invisible world of God. And in this operation of expressing the invisible world of the spirit in accessible, intelligible terms, you are the masters....

This, then, is my theme. It is necessary to re-establish friendship between the Church and artists....

But though we have always been friends, we must admit that often our relationship has been strained. I wonder whether I should say it? You have, as artists, somewhat abandoned the friendship: you have gone far afield to drink at other fountains seeking to express other things.... Sometimes you seem to forget the fundamental canon of your consecration to communication. We do not know what you are saying and sometimes you do not know it yourselves. The result is the language of Babel and confusion. We do not have the happiness of knowing what it is you wish to express, we are surprised, repelled, and then lose interest.

But I must be sincere and even daring. We admit that we, too, are to blame. We have imposed on you as a first canon that of conventional imitation—on you who are creators, vivacious people, alive with new ideas and innovations. We say this is our canon and you must adapt yourselves to it: this is our tradition and you must be faithful to it: these are our models and you must follow them: these are the roads and you must walk along them.

We have placed these shackles on you. For this I am sorry and ask your pardon. But more, in a way we have abandoned you....[8]

8. Pope Paul VI, "Allocution to Italian Artist in Sistine Chapel at the Artists' Mass, May 7, 1964." *The Pope Speaks*, v. 9 (1964): pp. 390–95.

If indifference, if not abandonment, shifted to an alliance, the religious community would emerge as a viable context for the processes and products of the artistic community's work, ushering in a relationship that would shift the parameters of today's aesthetic experiencing.

What are the parameters of an aesthetic experience? An understanding of them is within reach through a leap of imaginative engagement. Pretend you are an artist walking along an uninhabited ocean beach at dusk. Suddenly you spot a stunning piece of driftwood. You are grasped by the way it appears to converge with the seamlessness of land and sky in this twilight hour. You crouch down, study it, pick it up, and, with a tear in your eye, race home intent upon preserving this fleeting moment of heightened insight. You inspect this piece of driftwood, poke and press it here and there with reverence. You brush away the sand, and wipe it ferociously. Finally, you take a soft piece of cloth, dip it into very grayed-down blue paint and rub it into the driftwood's cracks and crevices, letting it seep and spill where it will. When it appears to capture the convergence of land and sky that captured you on your walk, you place it in the center of your table, ensconced in a pile of deep blue material reminiscent of the sea that cast it forth in the first place.

But suppose I come to visit you. I walk through your front door and spot the same piece of driftwood you did. This time, it's on your table. I say to myself, "Good heavens, that's awful, tacky beyond belief. It's outrageous. How could you have painted it and stuck it on that dreadful piece of shiny material?"

Also, suppose a professor from the academy, let us call him Professor Formalist, is with me when I walk through your front door. As I'm thinking these thoughts to myself, he walks over to the table, looks at your creation, and says, "Hmmm, interesting. A monochromatic color scheme, subtle shift of values, a deliberately textured surface, a relationship of shape to the framing device of the cloth. Its formalist properties are compelling."

Then, out of nowhere, in zooms your Great Aunt Bessie. When she spots the creation, she sashays over to the table, plucks the piece of driftwood from the material, marches straight out your back door, and plunks it in your garden as an ornament.

What we have in this vignette are four distinct happenings related to an aesthetic experience. In each instance, one aspect has primacy. When you as artist took home the piece of driftwood and intentionally worked on it, you, the artist, had primacy. In the second instance, when I visited and was repulsed by your effort, I, the viewer, had primacy. When Professor Formalist confronted it, the work had primacy in a very particular way; its syntax was readable. In the fourth instance, Aunt Bessie made the context primary. By removing it to the garden, she returned it to the outdoors where, perhaps, it most logically belongs. Thus, we have artist-artwork-viewer-context; these are the four parameters of an aesthetic experience.

If the religious community functioned as a solid and predictable context, the dynamics between the parameters of aesthetic experiencing within our culture would shift significantly. Such a shift hinges upon the religious leadership's acknowledgment of that which the historical evolution of art teaches us. Asserting the church and seminary as established contexts requires widespread conviction and courage to explore and find ways. Compelling needs within both the arts and religious communities suggest that now is the time.

Years ago I participated in a small symposium convened in a remote but gorgeous spot in Washington. I sat around a table with a handful of theologians, feeling like a token artist. The discourse was going nowhere, and tensions were high. Lush woods drowned in snow pressed against the windows. I nervously suggested a walk, knowing something they did not. Shivering towards nowhere, my disgruntled colleagues trudged. Then we spotted them, a ragtag bunch in the woods. Only I knew they were ceramic artists. There, the artist's bent figures reached deep into the snow, below which a hidden firing had taken place. In an instance, sputtering and smoking pots appeared in their hands made enormous by asbestos gloves. In a halo of steam, the pots' fired forms silhouetted against the stark white snow. Entranced, we watched. Their beauty bewitching, this spectacle of unearthed vessels triggered thought processes enabling comprehensive discourse. Thereafter it flourished. So did the questions.

Would the history of the church be better understood if students, when studying early church doctrine, encountered the victory arch mosaics of 5th century Santa Maria Maggiore? There the triumph of orthodoxy, expressed through the complex concept of Mary as Theotokos, is visualized.[9] Would students appropriate differently early church history if they encountered the great manifesto of the approaching Council of Trent through visual means, as exemplified in Michaelangelo's *Last Judgment*? By not engaging these works, do we in fact secularize our history and fall with the masses who, when gazing upon these masterpieces, no longer think the subject, but think art? For those for whom the Christian vision was central, do we ignore them as if their visions were not central, as if the inherent religiosity of their work was unimportant? By re-establishing them, do we re-establish ourselves?

What does a leap of faith require? Does spiritual maturity reside in the person who is unaccustomed to transcending limits, a hallmark of the creative act? Can aspirations for wholeness of personhood be realized in an environment weak in opportunities giving wings to the imagination? How, in fact, is imagination dealt with in theological education?

Engaging such questions enlivens one's conviction to establish the church and seminary as context. In considering context, remember that the parameters of aesthetic experience involve artist, artwork, viewer, and context. Remember that the relationship between these parameters has shifted through time and will continue to shift. Today, the artist and his or her work dominate the equation. Artists go to their studios and project their interior landscapes and then ask them to fit. The fit is negotiated for the most part through exhibition in a dealer-run gallery. It is the chief context, although an intermediary one, for today's artist. In our market-driven society, the artist and his or her work are distanced from the work's final context by the dealer who lies in between. Accustomed to receiving a 40%–50% commission based on the asking price of the artist's

---

9. Theotokos: Bearer of God.

work, the dealer, as the artist's agent, influences, if not dictates, the viewer's choice of an artwork. Therefore the dealer often plays a major role in determining an artwork's final context, whether it is a home, an office space, or other commercial setting. Galleries populate our cities like dense pushpins on a map. Viewers, from ultra casual browsers to deadly serious collectors, seek the gallery scene.

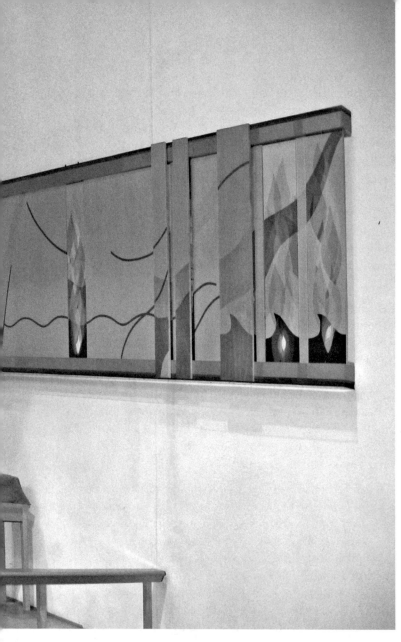

What would happen if the dynamics between the four parameters of an aesthetic experience were adjusted and resembled equality of attention? What would happen if the church took seriously its role as context and acted accordingly? If the religious community were to align itself with the art-making enterprise, several consequences would follow. For one, less art would reside in its own temple—the gallery or museum—a particular context now making possible the deification of art. In the gallery or museum, the catalogue provides the guide to a liturgy of adoration, lifting up and legitimizing the prophetic power of its resident works. These contexts are not the only ones wherein aesthetic disclosures dazzle viewers with truth-telling insights. Similar insights erupt in the concert hall. When the music heard transcends itself because each instrument contributes to a sound greater than the sum of its parts, the soul soars. In the theater, when actors and audience connect, additive presence illumines immaterial essence; flickering glimmers of truth unfold through the play's acted-out script. Be mindful that these manifestations resemble those that erupt in religious ritual. Art and religion are siblings.

Remember that much art of the past—tapestries, quilts, public sculpture, painted triptychs, icons, tomb walls of hieroglyphics, frescoed walls, mosaic floors, murals, and illuminated books bearing miniature painting—evolved from contextual relevancy.[10] Now some of this art of the past resides in museums where proper lighting, eye-level contact, and controlled temperature promote aesthetic contemplation. Alongside of it is modern and contemporary art. In this primary and pristine context, a consequence of today's time, such art is seen as autonomous and enshrined.

Changing patrons and ideologies tying art to its time of origin have brought us to this moment wherein much modern and contemporary art is unfathomable and indefinable for many. It is why some suggest that art-making is in a state of anarchy today. Certainly it exists for its own sake. But why shouldn't it? Understand that its autonomy is an evolutionary phenomenon. Next time you confront a complex work of art, ask, "How are you?" instead of "What is it?" Think of it as an offering of its own kind. Contemporary art's proclamation of its right to be is also a reflection of its eruption within a time placing the acquisition of experience, undifferentiated experience, at the center of living.

The thought of pleasing an audience, much less a handful of viewers in a church, is anathema to current thought. Further-

---

10. Triptych: a painting, relief sculpture, or wood carving in three panels side by side.

more, if the formalist properties of an artwork are very good, all sorts of content are justified. Remember Andres Serrano's *Piss Christ* and Robert Mapplethorpe's photographs of homoerotic imagery. Following a discussion of a Mapplethorpe photograph, Ellen Goodman wrote: "Show me somebody who can look at that photograph and think about the composition, symmetry, the classical arc of the liquid, and I'll show you someone with an advanced degree in fine arts."[11]

The dynamic between artist, artwork, viewer, and context is so elastic that content of high shock-value is trumpeted in the press and rewarded in the marketplace.[12] Consequently, such works and their attendant press cause the religious community to explode. Let these works stand as cogent examples of free speech. Rather than erupt, consider supporting and trumpeting powerful works of value, instead of only fussing when flustered. Content of high shock-value, like that which resided in *Piss Christ*, should have stood as a wake-up call to the church had the culture of the church been informed regarding contemporary art. *Piss Christ* made an important statement. Serrano's evocative photograph of a submerged crucifix in a see-through container of his urine proclaimed the dying of religious belief as evidenced in the contemporary irrelevancy of ecclesial symbology, most especially the cross. Take note of its meaning, and ignore it if it offends you. Nothing less than the value of artistic freedom is at stake.

A few years ago at the Brooklyn Museum in New York City, the explosion over Chris Ofili's *The Holy Virgin Mary*, an icon-like work with facial features evocative of his Nigerian ancestry, caused the same kind of ecclesial eruption because of applied elephant dung. Rather than berate and attempt censorship, expend energies seeking insights relevant to the contemporary art scene. He found dung an interesting material following a trip to Zimbabwe. About his *Holy Virgin Mary* he said:

11. Ellen Goodman, *Art's Linguistic Battle*, Boston Globe Newspaper Co., October 7, 1990.

12. The press continues to herald to the reader that human waste is a medium of artistic expression. "THEY DO KNOW SQUAT ABOUT ART," reads a May 19, 2005, headline of a *Washington Post* article. Its subtitle reads, "AT AUCTION BIDDERS ARE NOT MOVED BY TOM FRIEDMAN'S FECES ON A CUBE."

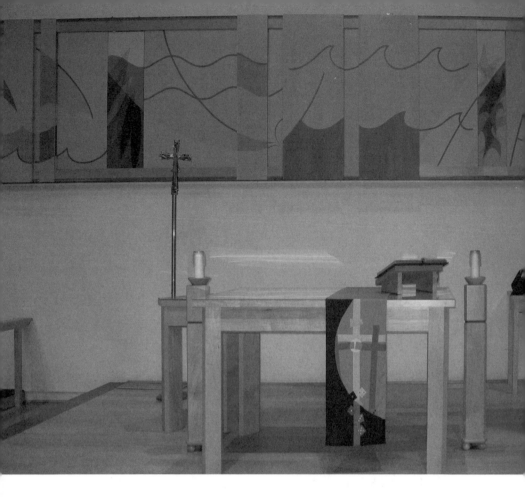

I don't feel as though I have to defend it. The people who are attacking this painting are attacking their own interpretation, not mine. You never know what's going to offend people. I believe in God, but I'm not dominated by it. The church is not made up of one person but a whole congregation, and they should be able to interact with art without being told what to think.[13]

An artist has an inalienable right to wed subject matter to material in any way, shape, or form imagined. Suspending a cloud of veiled censorship over an artist's head stifles possibility. This is a worse outcome than an occasionally disruptive work, disputed outrageously.

---

13. *The New York Times*, September 28, 1999.

Self-expression is at the core, if not is the purpose, of present day art-making. Artists and curators of contemporary exhibitions consider it a legitimate goal to shock the viewer. In fact, exhibitions are promoted to mine the controversial nature of some of their works. When a particular work or exhibition offends a category of people by assaulting its core value(s), viewers can self-select. Let these occasions be a time to listen, learn, and discuss what art is and what good is art.

Remember, as a consequence of viewing works of art as objects of perceptual contemplation, we have separated them in distinct ways. We erect buildings with the right kind of lights, proper temperature and humidity control, hanging devices for eye-level contact, and discrete divisions for works of separate periods, styles, and so forth. This is appropriate for modern and contemporary work, and work whose context is damaged or lost. In such buildings, we also house the very art that at one time had a different relationship to viewers because it was in its intended context. Now we treat the work autonomously. Its most important feature is its appeal to aesthetic contemplation.

Why not broaden the artist's experiential base, conceding the fact that for many in the church, the artist is the stranger? Never mind. We in the church proclaim the Living Word, from which comes the vision of Koinonia, the repeated welcoming and embrace of the other as other.[14] Scripture is replete with examples. "Love the sojourner therefore; for you were sojourners in the land of Egypt."[15] "Do not neglect to show hospitality to strangers, for thereby some have entertained angels unawares."[16] Respectful of this otherness, might the church embrace rather than smother the artist? In this paradigm, identity is not suffocated, rather all are enhanced by encounter. A Dallas minister says:

> I really think we have much in common. I think artists are concerned about saving the human spirit, creating the good community....

---

14. Koinonia: Greek word meaning communion, fellowship, common life; community produced by the Holy Spirit.
15. See Deuteronomy 10:19.
16. See Hebrews 13:2.

> that's the same thing I try to do.... If the art community and the religious community ever got together, it would be one of the most powerful unions that could happen in our world.[17]

The work of the artist and the work of the church are inexorably bound. Both seek a response, a transformation of thought in those who come to see and enter to hear. The work of the church is not about balancing what is with an infusion of the spirit of God. Rather it is about leveling what is with the Word and thus raising what is anew. Similarly, the work of the artist bears witness to a mysterious transcendence of what was by tearing up, distorting, shattering, and scattering raw material into radically new configurations. They cohere in their conjuring up of startlingly sustaining thought. Neither reproduces the visible. Both make visible, obliquely and suggestively, utterances of truth-telling. The unseen becomes seen, and we are sustained.

When art and art-making become embedded in the religious community, work side-by-side, look at each other face-to-face, and listen to each other, each helps the other do its work. Without the arts, theological proclamation is truncated. With the stimulus of critical questioning, art-making is enhanced. Both the product and the process of art-making belong in the context of the church and its educational institutions.

---

17. Alberta Arthurs and Glenn Wallach, editors, *Crossroads: Art and Religion in American Life* (New York: The New Press, 2001), p. 271. This book contains an excellent discussion of controversy in particular contexts and intersections of art and religion in wide contexts.

CHAPTER TWO

Mediating the Word

No longer is theologizing through the language and structure of philosophical discourse alone adequate to the task of bringing us to, or keeping us in, a love affair with God. Organized religion in the West has participated in its own demise by allowing propositional language dominion. The spoken word has reigned, limiting our access to scriptural truth.

Nevertheless, it is an established fact that the human family persists in yearning for encounters with the Holy.

> O God, you are my God, I seek you,
> my soul thirsts for you;
> my flesh faints for you;
> as in a dry and weary land
> where there is no water.[18]

A lived experience of the Holy comes in many guises: conversion, ascetic practices, mystical experiences, visions, prayer experiences, meditation, faith journeys, etc. Today a restless search for spirituality, for lived experience of the Divine, flits about the fringes of modern culture. We know that individuals experiment with spiritual techniques, spiritual guides, psychics, and occultism to access the "mysterious." We also know the casualties brought on by cultic practices and drug-induced experiments.

Christian spirituality is one that binds us particularly to a Triune God. We are led through the power of the Holy Spirit to meet the Jesus of history, the Christ of faith, the face of God. Within this Trinitarian framework, there are innumerable ways to

18. See Psalm 63:1.

31

encounter the Triune God. Schools of spirituality have sprung up through the ages, bearing names identifying them with the charisma and viewpoints of their founders: Benedictine, Celtic, Franciscan, Jesuit, Carmelite, Reformed, Wesleyan, etc.

Spiritual traditions generated through worldwide Christianity, its Orthodox, Catholic, and Protestant manifestations, emphasize differing practices enabling encounter with divinity. They exist on a continuum ranging from those that advocate mystical union through the elimination of sensual engagement to those that foster an experience of the sacred through the particularities of an image.

In Orthodox traditions, a lived experience of the Holy is known through meditation before an icon, considered a window on divinity. This practice constitutes a particular way by which an image serves. Historically, who is imaged with what specific attributes, as well as how the image is prayerfully painted layer by layer according to its prototype, has been governed by sets of rules. In Orthodox churches, the chancel and surrounding walls shimmer in a hierarchical arrangement of gold-leafed splendor with Holy personages and visages inviting the worshiper into the heavenly realm.

In this regard, the Quaker spiritual tradition is diametrically opposed to the Orthodox spiritual tradition. Lying in-between are a vast variety of means that rely on an image or imaging imaginatively to usher in a lived experience of the Holy.

Artists' encounters with these varying spiritual traditions have left an imprint on their work. Fra Angelico, a deeply pietistic practitioner of Dominican spirituality, painted frescoes of serene beauty.[19] El Greco painted extravagant images of biblical narratives informed by his scriptural meditations and spiritual practices legislated by the founder of the Jesuit movement. Rembrandt worked within the Reformed Tradition, dredging the deep psychological facets of biblical personalities whom he portrayed with disarming clarity. Van Gogh worked from a God-intoxicated mindset. The passion with which he painted paralleled that which motivated Ezekiel to eat the scroll.[20]

---

19. Fresco: the art of painting on freshly spread moist lime plaster with water-based pigments
20. See Ezekiel 3:1–3; Revelation 10:9–10.

Varying spiritual practices and/or a religious upbringing continue to inform a multitude of artists working today. However, the imprint of these influences is mostly veiled, unless unmasked by an astute viewer, sympathetic peer, or savvy critic. The network of art departments in Christian colleges and universities across the U.S. keeps alive the inherited conviction that religious sentiment is expressible in aesthetic form. Art stood and continues to stand as a corrective to the primacy of words as a way of mediating the sacred. It provides us an intuitive way of knowing, giving the Living Word a venue through which its voice is heard. The God who woos us comes through encounter. The plethora of great art that has endured the test of time is testimony to its mediation of transcendental spiritual sensibility.

Compelling contemporary testimony linking art and spiritual yearning appeared in the context of the preliminary hearings of the Yugoslav War Crimes Tribunal. On a daily basis the head of the eleven judges of the Yugoslav War Crimes tribunal listened to atrocities described. Asked how he, the judge, kept from going mad, his face lit up a bit. "Ah," he said with a smile. "You see, as often as possible I make my way over to the Mauritshuis Museum, in the center of town, so as to spend a little time with the Vermeers." As the judge put it, Vermeer's paintings reflect "a centeredness, a peacefulness, a serenity."[21]

Vermeer's work subjectively verifies for the judge what it means to be human. Standing before the work and giving it primacy, he imaginatively participates in the contemplation of it. Receiving insights, he dialogues with it. The work keeps disclosing itself (a sign of its greatness), charging the space between the two with translucent exchanges of meaning.

Take heed of our artistic heritage, of its role in disclosing the numinous.[22] The evolving modernist notion that art is best when serving only itself (now, aesthetic autonomy is crucial to arts value), rode in on the heels of Reformed theology. Together they perpetuate a chronic cycle of separation, divorce, and occasional

---

21. Lawrence Weschler, "Reflections: Inventing Peace," *The New Yorker* 71 (37) (Nov. 20, 1995): 56–64.
22. Numinous: filled with a sense of the presence of divinity; Holy.

remarriage between the arts and the Church. However, the historical antagonism and heated rhetoric between these two need not eclipse the possibility of a new and sustaining relationship. In fact the liturgical renewal movement of recent decades should contribute to a reunion—prayerfully, an enduring one.

A resounding factor evident in the chronic cycle of separation between art and religion preventing an aesthetic mediation of the Word is the church's mistrust of the sensual. I am reminded of this when I am in Wesley Theological Seminary's art studio glancing through its double doors, which open onto the hallway.[23] Occasionally a student will pass by, visibly stiffening, turning away his or her head, and averting his or her sight. This follows a quick, obviously surreptitious peek. The smell of turpentine wafting down the halls, the dance of colors arousing the sensibilities, or the passionate exuberance evident in the abundance of unfinished sculptures jammed near one another assault their sense of order and testify to the arts' sensual, earthy, and physical character. This turning away is lodged in the hierarchy of a body/spirit split which perpetuates a distrust of the sensual.

Nevertheless, the arts are for evocation, and sometimes for the shimmering embodiment of the One, the One who is the Beautiful, the True, and the Good. The triad of Beauty, Truth, and Goodness, a cornerstone of the church, signals a profound relationship of interpenetrating reality. Pretty, Reproducible Empirical Data, and Responsible Action do not. The former coheres as a single reality, while the latter is no more than a triad of separate parts. Beauty yields depth; pretty is superficial. Beauty, in its disarming intensity, binds the onlooker with the apprehension of that from which it emanates, the good and the true. Think how the glory of a radiant sunset, an instance of supreme beauty, penetrates our being. We perceive beauty as the emanating power of that which is true and that which is good. Beauty is the means through which the *mysterium tremendum* is encountered.[24]

---

23. Wesley Theological Seminary is a United Methodist Seminary located in northwest Washington, DC.

24. This term refers to the unfathomable mystery associated with that which points to the Holy, causing those who experience such an encounter to stand in awe. In applying the definition of symbol found in chapter 5, beauty is the symbol of the *mysterium tremendum.*

Several passages of scripture affirm the concept that beauty is of God. "Ascribe to the LORD the glory due his name...worship the LORD in holy array."[25] Glory is beauty's radiance, its dazzling, resplendent, and luminous characteristic. Holiness and beauty (other translations of the same text read, "In the beauty of holiness") bind substantively. The latter imparts awe, the former imparts mystery. Glory appears not only in things that are beautiful, but also in relationships with integrity, whether with God, self, or others. The Lord tells Job, "Deck yourself with majesty and dignity; clothe yourself with glory and splendor."[26]

---

25. 1 Chronicles 16:29; see also Psalms 29:2 and 96:8.
26. Job 40:10.

The central tenet of our faith states that God was incarnated in the person of Jesus. This is a revelation not only of the Word but also of the Image of God. Art in the context of sacred space actualizes the language of Incarnation through material means. This statement is crucial to welcoming aesthetic forms as mediators of the Word.

How does a numinous disclosure in ecclesial space heighten the crossing over into an experience of the sacred? How does a work of art bring another to his or her knees? My sense of how art transcends itself, of how the intermediate space between an art work and a viewer resonates with the possibility of luminous religious insight rests upon three variables. These set the possibility for triggering a flash of the sublime between work and viewer and determine the "how" of the relationship between art and the Holy.

The first variable regards the quality and truthfulness of the art work. The former aspect often emotes as a consequence of disciplined practice in the particular medium of expression. The latter aspect emerges when an artist pays attention to the radical particularity of his or her own experience. When the artist casts it into an aesthetic statement, the possibility of something approaching large-scale recognition gets said. Generally speaking, the more the artist goes to the edge to risk a conceptual leap by plumbing the depths of his or her knowing, the greater the likelihood this artist will express a common chord through his or her work. An art work does image, convey, and preserve, through its particular imprint and markings, the truth of its creator's experience.

Artists extract the essence of things, not representing the visible but making visible. Artists pound and hammer, paint and cut. Material is transcended because a penetrating consciousness is at work on it. The slice of life that originally captured the artist's attention is elevated. As the creative process unfolds, a new synthesis presents itself. Yes, art is the articulated metaphor of an engaged perception. What was originally a dim perception, observation, or issue has been shaped into a work through which the other is invited to find meaning. Never knowing we rely on a work of art until it appears, the artist's work says, "Stop, relevancy is reigning here."

The second variable regards the context in which the work resides. The logical consequence of acknowledging art's capacity to mediate the mysterious, to beckon us through the power of inbreaking numinosity, is to allow it to live in the Church. Churchgoing people already are predisposed to a sacramental view of life. They are attuned to finding the invisible in the visible. That is why the church as context is cogent. When a work of art is seen within a church, the viewer very likely will be predisposed to looking at it intently, whether it is representational, abstract, or non-objective. Of course, if it resonates through representational imagery (resemblance to external appearance), the return of the prodigal son for instance, the space between the work and believing viewer already is charged with the possibility of divine-human encounter. And as a consequence, less intentionality of focus is required of the viewer.

The third variable regards the conceptual capability of the viewer, whose experience and education or lack thereof predisposes him or her to see in particular ways. Imagine a non-objective work of art (lack of resemblance to external appearance), a work in which there is no recognizable subject matter, painted in a triptych format at the altar. The three separate rectangles on which the artist paints is this work's only tie to traditional religious painting found at the altar centuries ago. Suppose the artist concocts a compelling set of formalist relationships between interconnected colors, contrasting values, ecstatic-like lines, interpenetrating shapes, and thick textures formed from

spontaneous, gestural brushstrokes of paint. This confrontation with mystery both literally (unrecognizable image) and symbolically asks the viewer to traverse the light and dark passages, experience the emotion of color, feel the flow of line and shape, and roam the unfamiliar. In other words, give it attention. Even viewers lacking the education and experience predisposing them to accept non-representational imagery might be jolted into recognition of the inexpressible when confronting such a work at or near the altar. There, the work is seen while verbal and musical proclamation is heard simultaneously. This context provides a setting more likely to catapult such viewers into a frame of mind open to a new discernment of the Holy. The power of the in-breaking insight might even bring these people to their knees.[27]

I witnessed broadside the reverential impulse that brings people to their knees. It was in the National Gallery of Art, not a church. I remember standing among the hordes in the presence of the Vermeers. Snow clogged the city streets of our nation's capital, and the gallery shut down because the government ran out of money. Still, people clamored to see the Vermeers. Quickly, private monies came forward to provide guards, and the wing of the museum housing his paintings reopened. Lines of people assembled each day in the dirty, crusty snow before daybreak.

In the people-packed exhibition rooms, men and women stood reverentially transfixed before Vermeer's images. A hushed silence reigned as precious epiphanies burst forth from these works. No wonder people go in droves to see major museum exhibitions. For good reason.

Contemporary images assault if not smother us, and we proclaim a visual world. Some say that the Church should accommodate itself to the fleeting, instantly-readable, illustrational imagery rampant in our culture. Our challenge, at a time when our congregations are thinking visually, is to reject the easily

---

27. Friedhelm Mennekes' *Triptychon: Moderne Altarbilder in St. Peter Koln,* or *Triptych: Modern Altarpieces at St. Peter's, Cologne* (Insel Verlag, Frankfurt, am Main und Leipzig, 1995) uses fluid text and large, full-color reproductions to detail fifty contemporary three-part works. Each work was installed for a discreet period of time between 1987 and 1995 in the apse above the altar in the late Gothic parish church of St. Peter's.

accessible, facile images that too often appear as saccharine and sentimental illustration. Visual art that invites people into the presence of God for encounter and engagement is a different matter. It communicates through nuance and suggestion, its power to endure arising from its obliqueness. The imagination is awakened in such an encounter of meaning-making possibility. Our capacity to see needs thoughtful reinvigoration, for it is now disoriented by the rampant plethora of trivial, depersonalized, and often degrading images emerging from technological culture. Many television commercials impose an unexamined expectation for slick and quick pictorial solutions. It is the obligation and contribution of each worshiping community to gather up the received tradition, filter it through contemporary experience, and give it back in an imaginatively iconic way unique to its time.

In its attempt to mediate a sense of the sacred, my work reflects the particularity of my views. Sensing the sacramental nature of existence, the physical and spiritual are not rent asunder. Reality is the penetration of the temporal by the eternal, the seeing in simultaneity of the sacred in the secular, the invisible in the visible. This way of seeing is clearly a manifestation of an informed faith, imagined into being by Scripture, tradition, and experience.

In its attempt to make mystery visible and accessible, my work is not about adding something new for its own sake. Rather it attempts to disclose some aspect through material encounter of a shared belief. This work is mediated through faith and rendered through service to the community as servant to their spaces. It makes no sense apart from its architectural contexts and community-charged environments where people seek a lived experience of the Divine. This work stands symbolically, signing an interpenetrating spiritual reality that discloses itself when the community worships together.

Visual transparencies abound, that is, the overlapping of shapes that allow one form to be seen through another. It is a design technique wherein thesis and antithesis equals synthesis. At the very least, the visual joining together of separate entities by designing overlapping forms creates an added motif, while simultaneously allowing the overlapped to be seen. The result-ing synthesis creates a visual luminosity, mysterious for those who see it, when in the ritual moment of worship a translucent Presence is mediated.

The environment in which a worshiping community convenes is not complete until the assembly gathers. Abstract and non-representational imagery is not only appropriate but also "addi-tive" in such space because its content comes into focus, is brought to light, when the Gospel is preached, the hymns sung, and the Eucharist celebrated.

We are given accessibility to religious truth in a multiplicity of forms. We recognize the seemingly infinite refractions of proclamations from the pulpit disclosing glimpses of the inher-ent truth of Scripture. As remarkable in their own way are the myriad works of art that make meaning out of God-given material reconfigured. In fact, sometimes there is no other way in which a particular disclosure can come to us than through an artistic process or product. It is important to say that revela-tions born by art and central to our faith not only reflect the Spirit of God in our time but also say that there are truths to be experienced by God's people that yield more readily and per-haps only to the artists' imaginations and unique creative processes. Open the doors. The health of the Church's procla-mation is at stake.

CHAPTER THREE

Reading Liturgical Space

*I*n your imagination, walk with me into a congregation's worship space. We will wander through it together, studying it from all angles, sometimes from the pews, other times from the aisles, always from the entrance as well as the chancel, and finally from the balcony. This activity stimulates focused seeing. We all look; few, however, notice the nuanced relationships (or lack of) between architectural parts.

This reading to empower seeing is a collaborative venture. Observe the dominant sight lines that traverse the space and the repetitive and echoing shapes found in volumes and voids (pillars, pews, and empty spaces). Discourse on how color creates movement in the space, and locate where the intensity of one hue hijacks the life out of another. Discuss the range of values present (relative relationships of lights to darks), and address the way in which textured surfaces of materials relate to one another. Speak to the issue of scale. When a visual accoutrement is woefully out of scale, observe it, and rectify it if possible.

Simultaneously begin systematic interrogation (others call it visioning), which starts out like this, "Have you thought about the possibility of…?" This process animates reflection, which in turn stimulates more ideas and questions. At the same time, a deeper understanding of the visual dimensions of the space is being inculcated in the minds' eyes of all present. This talking process unmasks ("well, I never did understand that!") layers of thought and complexity ("the last member of the family who gave this is still living"). From this shared communication of musings and information gathering, possible visible concepts/ solutions framed by the original inquiry are evoked.

Reading ecclesial space enables the construction of a design framework within which a site-specific artist can create. For instance, if commissioned to create a set of liturgical banners, their eventual size, shape, placement, and way of hanging (against or angled to the wall as single entities or units of twos or threes, etc.) is determined entirely by the dictates of the space. Also the banners' colors will not only collaborate with but will often echo those found in the space. If commissioned to create paraments, their eventual size and shape is determined entirely by the configuration of surface planes, lines, and breaks evident in the chancel furniture. If, for instance, the season is Lent, and its designated liturgical color is purple, search until a harmonious shade or tint of purple is found. When a right relationship is achieved, optical visual harmony results. If commissioned to create a reredos for the space, look once again at the chancel design structure. The design of the reredos must relate to, if not, result from a recasting and echoing of scale and parts indigenous to the architectural structure in which it will reside.[28]

Once I missed reading (seeing) a crucial architectural element in a liturgical space. Well into a three-year effort working in that space, it never occurred to me that I had not noticed a detail in what I was accustomed to seeing. But that is precisely what happened, and its consequence had repercussions. It also proved the age-old adage that creating art is all about making one's mistakes work. It is for this reason I tell the story.

Volunteers had completed the needlepointed sections of a commissioned 25' by 10' chancel reredos. One night several hours into a deep sleep, I was caught unaware. I awoke suddenly realizing that I had ignored the 18" wide by 14" high by 12" deep high altar's pedestal extension on which sits a 5'2" brass cross. I had planned a seamless joining straight across of the tapestry reredos' 10' bottom edge with the high altar's top edge. Aware that this extension would hide one of the volunteer's needlepointed contributions now complete, I panicked. What was I to say to her? Besides, how could I have missed seeing something so obvious?

---

28. Reredos: a screen or decorated part of a wall behind an altar.

Also in my head were another volunteer's words. With a loomingly large mistake to fix, her words, reminding me of her mortality, turned into a silent litany. She, more than 80 years old, was one of the regulars of a stalwart group of volunteers who had come two years earlier to the studio at 1:00 pm several days a week. For three tedious months they transcribed designs into the colors of yarn available, thereby aiding in the fabrication of one half of a full-scale color model. My doorbell would ring, and our sons' undisciplined golden retriever would herald their arrival. I, with heart pounding, would envelop this volunteer, whom I feared would be knocked over by my unruly dog. Simultaneously I would suggest to her in a veiled sort of way that perhaps our task was too tiring for her and hint to her that she consider withdrawing from it. In an unruffled voice, she would respond, "Why dear, absolutely not. I just hope to live long enough to see this work done." Now, two years later, teetering between life and death, my mistake threatened the fulfillment of her persistent plea.

Thankfully, several days after my rude awakening, the insight arrived. I designed a dedicatory wooden plaque resembling the wooden tracery housing the needlepointed sections of the reredos. In it, the section that otherwise would have been hidden by the altar's pedestal extension was placed. It resides on a wall nearby to the reredos like a sentinel, its separation a mark of distinction for its maker.

A short time after the installation and celebratory dedication of the reredos, our faithful friend who feared she would not see the completed work died.

Reading corporate spaces where temporary liturgical work will reside also necessitates looking critically, closely, and carefully. The goal in studying a space is always the same, regardless of its size or place. There is no difference in looking at a 5,000-seat convention center, its lobby, one of its meeting rooms, or, for that matter, a hotel lobby. Create a compatible work, large or small.

Within a design framework or construct, infinite possibilities for creative expression abound. Orson Welles said, "The enemy of art is the absence of limitations."[29] Paradoxically, within a

---

29. http://www.brainyquote.com/quotes/quotes/o/orsonwelle109697.html (accessed November 14, 2005).

constraint unlimited expressive possibilities exist. Paradoxically, I am empowered by the commissioning process, which other artists consider a restraint and call an obstacle to self-expression.

The objective is to stimulate thoughtful reflection on how tradition and innovation might march hand in hand. The artist's job is to explicate the difference between creativity and originality, the latter an icon of the modern age. As such, its reverence has eclipsed the notion that a creative edge can be legitimately expressed through a tradition that is dealt with innovatively. By analogy, musical improvisation works this way. In fact, tinkering and toying with traditional practices, especially those of liturgy, ensure a healthy, living, and ongoing tradition. The artist's purpose is to help the community grasp the nuanced difference between a design concept that would compete with the environment (thereby diminishing it) over and against a design concept that would enhance and amplify the environment (thereby showing it to be more fully what it is).

While the intent of an art work in liturgical space is to focus attention on the action of the worshiping community rather than to become the object of attention, there is plenty of room for innovation. The committee discovers through this reflective process with the artist that the work will assist in the moment when Word, sacrament, and song mingle to achieve an instance in which transcendence occurs. Work of this kind is always particular, specific to a particular congregation, in a particular time. Liturgical art is absolutely contextual. Sometimes, it does not make much sense apart from its place of habitation.

Whether a congregation's interest is in a visual explication of the liturgical seasons, a visual interpretation of a passage of scripture central to the community, or a visual portrayal of an overarching theological theme, the process of exchange is the same. Only the site is different. Worship spaces differ radically in size and style. Although many Christians have in common the lectionary text, liturgical action, and commitment to service, they do not have in common architectural space. The vast variety of geographic locales in which an equally vast number of architectural styles proliferate inspires differing artistic responses reflective of their dissimilarities.

Much is learned on both sides when the liturgical space is seen, studied, and read together. Congregants begin to imagine abdicating received intractable notions about what is "appropriate" in ecclesial space. They may consider commissioning a design but fabricating it themselves. [30] Such a community building venture recognizes special skills belonging to certain congregants. If such an undertaking ensures, the work becomes the work of the people. Congregants might also discuss the idea of temporary versus permanent work while continuing to address the continuum between traditional versus more innovative solutions. The exchange between artist and congregation, no matter the variety and complexity of issues raised, provides the artist with the know-how to conceive a design solution. It takes its dictates from the space and community in a spirit of collaboration. This exchange also provides the community with thorough knowledge of the artist.

More often than not, "visual noise" is encountered. Another word for this noise is "clutter"—too much of too many unrelated things. Sometimes visual noise is rampant. An overabundance of items unnecessary to liturgical function often proliferates. Items of inappropriate scale are common, as are discordant design relationships between catalogue paraments and chancel furniture. Sometimes a symbol, such as the cross, proliferates. The profusion of a single symbol not only negates its power, but it also achieves a visually noisy environment by reducing the symbol to knick-knack and ornamentation. It is synonymous with a preacher who clutters with too many words in an attempt to drive home the message. Essence, that which lingers like mist, is lost in both instances.

Commonly the American flag and the state flag in the chancel add to the clutter.[31] The chancel is an inappropriate place for their display; that which they symbolize is extraneous to chancel function. Visual noise, while not consciously acknowledged by many, is just as distracting as auditory noise. Imagine airplanes flying overhead during worship every three minutes en

---

30. Fabricate: to make; to construct with an aesthetic sensibility.
31. A more appropriate place for their display is the back of the sanctuary, the narthex, or the fellowship hall.

route to a nearby landing strip. Both kinds of noise assault—one the visual sensibility, the other the auditory sensibility. Visual noise is a common problem for churches. Because of the egalitarian nature of church communities (everybody has a say and thus a contribution), this reality, while explainable, is regrettable.

Occasionally, astonishing findings occur, such as those at a large, visually lavish, and elaborate church on St. Charles Street in New Orleans, Louisiana. Each time I went to the back of the sanctuary and looked towards the raised chancel platform, the back wall of which was marked by a series of pillars in relief about 18" apart, I was jarred, agitated. Something about the many relatively narrow, stained wood surfaces between the cream/colored pillars unsettled me. They appeared flat, tonally undifferentiated, unlike real wood. On the other hand, each time I looked from the middle of the sanctuary or from the edge of the platform, the stained wood surfaces were adequate.

The abundance of powerful visual delights (imported Italian brocade) coupled with the domineering quality of the pillars at close range in fact eliminated the panels' odd appearance seen from the entrance.

When the consultation was complete and committee members had left, I returned to the sanctuary alone. The enigma had me in its grip. I entered at the back, stopped, and peered towards the chancel. Intensely agitated, I marched straight to the platform, skipped up the steps and squinted at the wood surfaces. Ten minutes later I was in the minister's office, telling him I thought it imperative for the church to remove all the contact paper simulating a wood surface between each and every pillar. Shaking his head from side to side, he mused, "It has been here for many, many years."

The artist should spend considerable time alone in the space (or in front of photographs following a weekend visit) tossing about ideas. The process of evolving a concrete solution requires meditation, study, and incubation time. Worship with the community, visit with them, and listen to them. A strong sense of their theological bent is gained over time as further communication ensues. Discovering who the community is, is as important as reading their space. Visual cues come from their environment; cues for content come from the congregation. The commissioned artist's way of working in an ecclesial context involves assessment of the issues, review of skills, acquisition of new skills deemed necessary, imposition of self-discipline, and implementation of ideas born from imaginative leaps between all aspects of the commission's parameters and what is merging under the hands. An artist must listen to his or her work.

CHAPTER FOUR

Transforming Space

*T*he artist's role in the transformation of ecclesial space ranges from tangential to central. An artist's singular work can induce a major change in the look of an environment. Or, the artist's work may contribute to a master plan devised by a liturgical design consultant who simultaneously solicits the work of several artists. A cavernous new cathedral necessitates a response that differs from the one dictated by a small, country church. Nevertheless, they share issues in common.

The transformation of ecclesial space is a complicated task because it necessitates the involvement of many. When a creative process (an act necessary for any transforming activity) submits to a democratic process, general opinion suggests that mediocrity will result. Seeking a solution invigorated, rather than handicapped, by the input of many necessitates some rules. Nobody gains if all are walking a tightrope because artist and community are in tension with one another.

Since the transformation of ecclesial space is of a collaborative character, education of all parties concerned is the essential ingredient for pursuing successful solutions. Much educational companioning of each venture is essential. Every aspect of a project undertaken to enhance communal space, ecclesial or not, must be vigorously explicated.

At our seminary, we have a tunnel that is 100' long and turns a corner. Everyone walks through this space, often to and from chapel services. The temperature drops upon entering the tunnel, and in the summer, mold creeps up its walls. Occasionally, the tunnel floods.

In the 1970's, an innovative student arrived one day with several gallon cans of paint purchased in a nearby hardware store. Thinking that her plan to paint Noah's ark in the tunnel was the perfect solution, she handed the $50 receipt for the paint to the academic dean. He balked, and she returned the paint.

In the 1980's, I petitioned the administration with a proposal to restore the walls and install lights to set off masterful ceramic relief sculptures of contemporary Stations of the Cross. They had been created and given to us by one of our artists-in-residence. This proposal would have enabled cast shadows resulting from directed lighting on the relief figures, progression of subject matter logically fitting the elongated space, the transformation of a dull space into a devotional space, and subtle physical discomfort induced by temperature change to be an asset in experiencing the thematic content of the stations. The solution was rejected due to lack of funds for lighting and minimal wall restoration.

In the 1990's Union Theological Seminary in Richmond, VA, sent one of its students for a two-semester sojourn at our seminary. He was an accomplished studio artist and college professor of studio art seeking practical experience integrating art with theology. Woong-Sik Timothy Chon and I peered down the tunnel and schemed. By now, the community was ripe for a transformative change. The failed attempts of the past had left their imprints.

Knowing from past experience how critical having an informed community is, I appointed a small, select committee from the faculty, staff, and student body. I solicited a polished, in-scale, full-color design concept from Chon, fashioned after the two of us had experimented with and decided upon a buon fresco technique as the medium of expression. The committee accepted our concept. Chon began his arduous task surrounded by an inquisitive, caring community and lovingly supported by his wife and three small children.

As fall progressed, Chon created cartoons (preparatory drawings) that combined Eastern and Western influences and tackled the inherent problems in this exacting technique of applying paint to a perfectly prepared wall of wet lime and plaster. At the moment of control with this process, Chon was catapulted into the abyss. His daughter Soh-Leen Sarah Chon, following 100 days of life just celebrated at her baptism, died suddenly in her sleep. Wracked by pain, grief, and anguish Chon returned week after week to the tunnel. Sometimes he labored productively, other times in vain, and mostly in solitary sadness.

In these initial weeks, buckets of seemingly black paint bonded to the wall. Colleagues passed through the tunnel in silence. I teetered between trust in Chon's process, my responsibility as kind friend and mentor (Chon needed the therapeutic benefits of painting), and the committee's threshold for a work radically different from the one proposed. No one said a word as they passaged through the tunnel, and some averted their stares at the wall being painted. The kind of preparation discussed above stood all of us in good stead.

In the ensuing months, Chon transformed our tunnel into the visual epic journey of a person moving through grief to hope. He put before us a monumental work of abstracted imagery bearing testimony to God's healing presence. Traversing one side of the 100' tunnel from floor to ceiling and a portion of the opposing wall seen upon entering at its turned end, Chon moved the imagery through the following eight themes: creation, mother and child, marriage of heaven and earth, lament, transformation, resurrection, reunion, and text (a handsome calligraphic rendering of Matthew 11:5).[32] Near the solitary panel of text, mounted on the wall, is a shelf lacquered in the oriental red that repeats the color of the molding outlining the top and bottom edge of the whole fresco. On this shelf sits a large book of empty pages in which a steady stream of anonymous prayers and reflections appear. Now, the tunnel is a place of healing. This venture necessitated a creative response from the artist and community alike. Says Chon, "God used the creative process of the fresco painting to shape Shalom."[33]

---

32. Karin Tunnell transcribed the scriptural text into a full-scale, calligraphic cartoon for the wall and assisted Chon in carving the text into the wall.

33. *Shalom* is the Hebrew word for peace with a surplus of meaning. Both a greeting and a blessing, it infers holistic well-being, both individual and collective.

Goethe, Schleiermacher and others have reminded us that it takes as much creativity to appreciate a work of art as it does to make it. For the gift and the essential inner meaning of all great works of art is that they inspire, activate and pass on the creative impulse. And here is the paradox of the artist: individual vision cannot be understood without the community that receives it, and the results of an artist's creative actions are meaningless without the community that has a use for them. Here is the socio-political dilemma of the model of the artist as an isolated, unique and individual genius that we have inherited today.[34]

I always commence an educational process when I attempt transformation of a space (or undertake a similar exchange in related ecclesial spaces) with members of the commissioning community. If my involvement with the community extends beyond the original consultation, whether it yields a finished work, a design, or an overall plan for visual renewal, I council the church to undertake a commitment to educate its entire body regarding all aspects of new work undertaken. An individual supported by a small cadre of committed persons constituted as a committee must take responsibility for this necessity.

The size of the church dictates the extent of educational activity necessary because its size determines the scope of transforming work undertaken. Usually, but not always, the larger the church body, the bigger the space and the more complex the project. Issues vary according to size. Nevertheless, the need is the same. Start by constituting a committee for the arts. Depending upon the politics of the church, it may have to be a subcommittee of the music committee, liturgy committee, worship committee, etc. If the subcommittee does its work well, eventually it will stand separate and autonomous.

---

34. "Reflections on The Image" by Bill Viola in *Art and the Spiritual.* Edited by Bill Hall and David Jasper (Great Britain: University of Sunderland Press, 2003) p. 2.

First, this committee must stand ready with answers to such questions as:

- What do artists share in common with us?

- Why is the presence of art important in ecclesial space?

- Is concrete, recognizable subject matter necessary?

- How do you evaluate the function of artwork in relationship to worship?

- What can we do to enable a quality work?

- How do we bring our congregation on board, invested?

Secondly, the committee explores the community's aesthetic needs and seeks solutions for these needs. Consider the whole ecclesial environment. In particular, do not rob or truncate the aesthetic dimension of Christian worship. In order that those who experience it are clutched by the grip of its proclamation, unable to shake it loose, empowered to serve and act rightly, inundate all the senses simultaneously. It is a glorious way to meet the One who gives us the vision, the vision of Shalom. Don't risk reduction. Risk exuberant color, startling imagery, discordant sound, a chancel drama, a poetic reading, and elements danced up the aisle.

In addition to educating the community, other cogent considerations command attention when transforming space. Fiscal responsibility, distinctions between product and process, traditional versus innovative solutions, permanent versus temporary work, and allowance for children's contributions are issues for consideration. The arts committee plays a critical role in explicating and negotiating these issues.

Fiscal capability varies greatly. Usually a small congregation of nuclear families has limited space and a small budget in contrast to an immense congregation with a large space and matching budget. The latter might undertake multiple commissions over time with artists using a variety of media (composers, sculptors, dancers, poets, actors, etc.) with compensatory fees gleaned from a budget earmarked annually for this endeavor. In contrast, the former might undertake a commission with a local artist in the neighborhood whom the church pays for materials only. My very first invitation to create a work for permanent liturgical use was in a small neighborhood Lutheran church. I accepted, and life was never the same afterwards.

Churches on the continuum between the very large and the very small will range in their financial ability, from the support of one artist's time and materials to the support of several design proposals in competition for a commission. Whatever the extent of the commitment, the arts committee's critical function is to ward off issues before they become intractable problems. The sudden appearance of something unexpected in communal space can be lethal. Contrary to popular myth, an educated and therefore invested congregation rejoices in the birthing of significant work. For this to happen, members of the arts committee, with clergy and other church leadership in tow, must continually inform the community of the twists and turns related to the artistic undertaking.

When the arts committee establishes a healthy rapport with the artist(s), then it negotiates a contract and finally circulates a steady flow of material related to the endeavor. Once an artist has been selected and stipulations negotiated, respect the artist's need for time. After disciplined listening to each other, after all the issues, concerns, requests, and dreams are on the table, give the artist autonomy.

The table re-opens for discussion at the time of the review by the committee of the intended solution, usually a design mock-up in scale and full color. Thoughtful inquiries, careful listening, and considered responses define the exchange. The people at the table are the original ones with no additions. At this juncture, the committee either approves the artist's work and chooses to proceed, negotiates changes, or terminates further work.

This juncture is critical for both the commissioning community and the artist. The former needs a clear, visual concept of what the artist intends to create. The latter needs to have a contractual arrangement wherein the fee structure provides remuneration for design work in the event its intended execution is terminated. Few understand how labor intensive is the task of creating an articulate design concept in scale.[35]

---

35. Parenthetically, my contractual arrangements vary according to each commission. I have no prescription. My contracts for works in military chapels looked, I imagined, like ones given to an electrician. My contracts from the church have been as precise as a roadmap and as simple as a letter signed by the senior pastor or chair of the supervising committee. For a more detailed description, see Kapikian, "The Art of Earning a Commission," *The Flying Needle: Ecclesial Design*, August 1987, p. 6–7.

There are multitudinous ways to transform space. Whether a community opts for changing works related to each liturgical season; an installation that lasts for one service or season; a permanent, fixed, and unchanging work; or some combination of all of these, think about giving visibility to the process undertaken to create them.

Historically, the church has engaged art as a product. Today it is also advantageous for congregations to engage art as process. Give space and visibility, if temporarily, to a painter, sculptor, composer, dramatist, dancer, poet, etc. While an artist is working on your church's commission, he or she in turn will engage the community. From the inception of the idea to the finished product, this companioning process enhances the possibility of congregational support, even advocacy, for the acquisition of art, and especially visual elements in worship. Music, the one consistent art form present in worship, exists not only as product (performance) but also as process (participatory hymn singing). Music has maintained its persistent presence in worship because it is primarily participatory.

By engaging art as process, congregations become more adroit at reading the nonverbal language of the visual. Its vocabulary is as alien to many as is an unfamiliar foreign vocabulary. How does one understand visual theological proclamation without a rudimentary grasp of its language? With it, artists speak. They tinker with a color's intensity, confound with a brash imbalance of shapes, blur boundaries between passages of value shifts, mess with meandering lines, and toy with textured surfaces. Whatever the artist's intention, giving visibility to his or her creative process is a community-enhancing experience. Through it, theological proclamation vis-à-vis this vocabulary becomes comprehensible. Decades of resident artists working in our seminary studio have disclosed the value of seeing and experiencing their processes.

The following words of world-renown architect Frank Gehry pinpoint the relationship of process to product in the context of community.

> For me and for the people that work for me, in a way what we do is less about the final product and more about achieving the final product, because that's what we spend all of our time doing. So aside from the fact that we all consider ourselves lucky that we're in a position to work with great clients and great consultants, what matters most is the process of doing all of it…. I sketch it out, once we know it will function then we start, sometimes with a crumpled paper but mostly with other materials, and we build model after model after model. We agonize about every little part of it, and I stare for hours and then I move something just a little bit, and I stare some more, and then slowly it starts to take shape. And the clients are around for all of this. They are a part of it, so we do it all together. Eventually we figure out where we are going…. And why do we do it? Because it's what we've chosen to do; it's what our experiences have led us to do and so we do it

to the best of our ability. And I guess sometimes we get it right.[36]

Whether the focus be on process or product, the transformation of worship space must consider the offerings of our children. Our children communicate naturally through the
non-verbal vocabulary of the visual (in fact they express themselves exuberantly until they are acculturated out of this capacity). The creation of temporary, evolving (an addition each
week building incrementally), or changing work for worship
offers insightful breakthroughs of meaning. As a congregation,
adults and children become accustomed to visual amplification, thriving on shifts between temporary versus permanent
and traditional versus innovative solutions. This dynamic processing keeps meaning-making alive. The key to its vitality
turns in the hands of the arts committee. Its members must be
attentive to options, innovative in risking unorthodox efforts,
and vigilant in their educational responsibilities on behalf of
community.

Lively thought is initiated when children's visual offerings, fresh
and spirited, transform space. Their painted, crayoned, or
drawn images created in response to passages of scripture, theological themes, a particular hymn, or a devastating event can
all be cast large, compatible to the scale of the space. Pull out
compelling images from an aggregate of children's paintings
and drawings, remove a face, a rain cloud, a family, etc. by trac-
ing them exactly as drawn. Then enlarge the images with an
overhead projector and transfer them to another surface. These
enlarged images can be carried as processional banners and
afterwards hung in clusters on the wall in the fellowship hall.

Consider the use of children's work in the sanctuary one week
out of each liturgical season. Enlarged images of children's work
in chancel space contrasted to their appearance on bulletin covers (or in the bulletins) or inside the covers of the attendance
pads in diminished scale is enchanting. So is seeing your children's images each liturgical season in the chancel. Accomplish

---

36. Museum of Contemporary Art, Los Angeles, *FOG: Flowing in all Direc-
tions,* quotation by Frank Gehry inside front cover. Circa Publishing,
2003.

this by mimicking the frontal surface of the chancel furniture with a thin piece of wood or foam core designed and finished as an integral part of the pulpit, lectern, or table. Once each liturgical season, tack your children's images to it. The furniture is protected, and the community rejoices in the whimsy of its children. Our children, now grown-up, might pass through the doors more often to see and hear had they heard and seen in their younger days their own expressive proclamations valued. Might routine have been colored by celebration?

I recall a charming transformation using the images created by children in what seemed like an already complete event. The Washington National Symphony under the baton of Hugh Wolfe sponsored an afternoon performance at the Kennedy Center for grade school children in the Washington, DC, Metro Area (District of Columbia, Maryland, and Virginia). One of the works programmed for the upcoming concert was Richard Strauss's *Till Eulenspiegel.*

Prior to the event, children were invited to submit, through their school systems, a picture interpreting one of the merry pranks of Till. Hundreds and hundreds of pictures arrived. About sixty, divided into categories based on Till's escapades, were photographed onto 35mm slide film. After all the musical pieces except the Strauss had been performed, Wolfe introduced *Till Eulenspiegel* by soliciting sounds from the drummers, the horn players, etc. descriptive of Till's escapades. The hall darkened, and *Till Eulenspiegel* commenced with a flourish. Simultaneously enormous projected pictures flashed onto the wall behind the players. Calibrated to the music and visually descriptive of it, the children's projected images kept pace with the story line. I was in the audience. I still remember vividly the uniform gasp from the crowd, the sitting up in the seats of hundreds. The children understood instinctively the nonverbal vocabulary. Two instead of one sensibilities were being inundated. It was a riveting moment.

Simultaneously, it struck me that much of church leadership has seriously underestimated the power resident in an aesthetic form. I now own the slides that were used in the concert. Periodically, I show them to my students with musical

accompanment as an example of what can be done. For instance, why not have our children paint a response to "All Things Bright and Beautiful"? Then scan the images digitally, and project them large as a centerpiece of an intergenerational event.

Whether the impetus comes from reminding myself of the spontaneous way children approach image-making or whether it comes from remembering all the interactive activity with a commissioning community, such thoughts propel me to the studio. Mostly, the sheer terror of a rapidly approaching deadline drives me to it.

Once in the studio, common process steps undergird how I approach transforming space. I tack photographs of the space against my work wall. I lay my folder containing notations I have made regarding the space (its colors, value differentiations, site lines, expectations regarding content, etc.) in the middle of my work table among the steadily growing heap of materials such as paper, pencils, color aid swatches, scissors, glue, etc. First I determine the dimensions of the completed work I wish to create, for instance of a reredos in the chancel or a wall work in the narthex. Then I proceed to draw scores and scores of "thumbnail" sketches, abbreviated and clumsy gropings that grasp at ideas. These small, initially vague scribblings force clarity of thought and eventually open the way to a visual resolution. As they grow more articulate, I draw in a larger scale, but always in a scale commensurate with the dimensions of the already conceived work. There is no point dreaming up a solution in different proportions than those already prescribed by the envisioned work. For instance, if my work when completed will be 4' by 8', it is a tactical error to design in a 3' by 6' format, no matter in what scale I am working (2" = 1' or 3" = 1', etc.).

Often I replicate in scale the entire wall or environment in a 2-D or 3-D model against which or in front of which the work will reside. Included are the details of the whole visual field. For instance, if the dossal cloth is surrounded by handsome molding that the community wishes to retain while simultaneously

replacing the dossal cloth with a more iconic representation, I create a solution that not only respects the design characteristics of the molding but also shows the molding in scale as part of the visual field.[37]

In my creative processes that attempt a material transformation of (or in) a space, the concerns foremost in my mind are whether or not the work emerging under my hands is theologically revealing, appropriate to the space, attentive to the community's thematic expectations, and forcing me to a new frontier. I insist upon self-imposed risk because its absence insures a recipe for mediocrity.

Memories of my reading of the space and my meetings with clergy and community linger. I engage in a contemplative kind of thought which is circuitous and inclusive. I struggle to create a work in which the visual elements of the space coalesce into a dynamic equilibrium. Grounded in a theological idea, I aim to achieve a heightened perception of the whole, created out of relationships of light and dark, figure and ground, dull and vivid intensities, patterns, and repetitions. This way of creating art is born out of community for the sake of community. It also necessitates:

> Nights without sleep and days
> that burn like a smoldering fire,
> Nerves with the ceaseless cry
> of wind in a tight-drawn wire—
> Years of this leaving me nothing
> but a handful of songs like these,
> That people think were happily written
> in an hour of ease.[38]

---

37. Dossal cloth: an ornamental hanging of rich cloth behind an altar
38. Sara Teasdale, "Nights without Sleep" song. Music by Garth Baxter.

CHAPTER FIVE

Reclaiming Symbols

*B*ooks on the subject of symbolism and symbol proliferate. They range from the obtuse, nearly incomprehensible, to the practical, bordering on the superficial. Descriptions and definitions abound. Paul Tillich gave a useful definition of symbol as that which "participates in the reality of that for which it stands."[39] Thus symbol brings back to life, empowering a re-living of that which it represents. The thoughts and emotions that "living" symbols evoke are triggered by no other means than through the symbols themselves.

The use of symbols is central to the work of the liturgical artist. Their use saves the church from the presence of work based solely upon the artist's privatized artistic projections. Symbolic representation is a catalyst for a particular reliving of experience important to liturgical function. Its purpose is to evoke from the worshiper a spiritual response that involves the mingling of mind and emotion caught up momentarily in a revelatory way of knowing. Symbolic representation greatly enhances the truth-telling capacity of myth, rituals, and stories through which religion speaks.

Our churches struggle in a culture dominated by a secularism rife with violence, competitiveness, and acts of degradation. In it, the world is ours, not God's. We may do with it as we like; God is absent from it. While unintended, much worship reinforces this world by its rootedness in entertainment rather than in liturgical distinction. The latter symbolizes through material embodiment a different world.

---

39. *The Dynamics of Faith*, planned and edited by Ruth Nanda Anshen. World Perspectives, vol. 10. NY: Harper and Brothers, 1957, p. 239.

The Protestant Reformation in part ushered in a corrective regarding a surplus of material embodiment, that is to say, of symbolic expression. Our problem is the opposite one. We must give birth to new symbols and divest our spaces of those tied to a bygone time (God as king). This cannot be done without the artist. This urgent need calls for a reformation of its own kind. Looking back fifty years, our American abstract expressionists had the courage of conviction to straddle chaos with paint and canvas, bequeathing to us symbolic works of angst and desperation.

An internationally acclaimed member of this group, Willem de Kooning sent a signal late in his life (approximately twenty-five years ago) that he hoped to receive a commission to create a religious work. [40] Shortly thereafter, he did. St. Peter's Lutheran Church in New York City commissioned a painted triptych for their altar. This famous artist visited the site and went to work in his Long Island studio. He painted a non-objective image relying on fluid lines of primary colors of varying widths and intensities that intersect, encircle, and disappear. In their aggregate, they yield a masterful work.

Meanwhile, the church was splitting in two, polarized by opposing points of view regarding this noteworthy commission. One side said that the art and architecture review committee's authority to grant such a momentous commission ignored channels of communication and authority within the church necessary to the process. The other side touted the fame of the artist. Owning a de Kooning would be efficacious for the church. This point of view further inflamed the other, whose prime mover was a noted scholar of liturgical studies. She voiced the view that "the finer the art piece, the less likely that the art can serve the assembly in its attention to the liturgy."[41] Cascading trains of thought from both camps

---

40. This desire was disclosed in an interview in *The New York Times Sunday Magazine*, November 20, 1983.
41. This quote and the information given here about de Kooning's work come from the following article: "A Willem de Kooning Triptych and St. Peter's Church" by John Cook, in *Theological Education*, Vol. XXXI, Number 1, 1994, pp. 59–73. For a thorough and erudite examination of all the issues, plus commentary on the issues, please see this entire article.

unleashed torrents of arguments, all before the work was seen. How could it be authentically encountered on its own terms when it did arrive? It could not.

A flawed process left all persons on both sides uninformed about particular aspects of the commission, including the place of the image within the history of worship, the relevance of context to art in culture, theological proclamation in non-objective visual format, and distinctions between product and process, which in this case precluded discourse with the artist by the community except for a few who negotiated with his representatives. The list goes on.

A donor was being sought to purchase the work for the church throughout the controversy. The artist's dealer had informed the church that the market value of the triptych was set at $1,000,000. Upon the triptych's completion, it arrived at the church for a "viewing" of several weeks, but was returned to the artist despite the fact that he had decided to donate it to the church.

This fiasco is worth noting, for it shows us that works of art are powerful, democratic process is critical in community negotiations, people are passionate about their churches, education is essential regarding the acquisition of artworks, and stewardship of funds concerns all churches.

What does this lamentable tale tell us about symbolism or lack thereof as we are accustomed to seeing it in a work of art? In point of fact, de Kooning's work was couched in a universal symbol of liturgical art, the triptych. Within its framework was his privatized interior landscape. Memories from long ago when he experienced churches as a young artist in Rome were conjured up in this work, which he called *Hallelujah*. Sadly, his triptych could not be seen independent of a swirl of hostile, preconceived notions brought to it. Regrettably, his triptych was not seen through an encounter in liturgy for an extended period of time. Had it been, it might have been seen as symbolic of the source and ground of our being.

Symbols that are visibly present and comprehended free the congregation from captivity to words. Think of the presence of visually vibrant, mysteriously translucent symbols as invitations, imparting a jolting sense of recognition and connectedness. They can flame into meaning and ring with clarity as they emerge to sight from a mysterious background of colors and shapes. However, if they appear trite, as if blatantly cut-out and pasted down, cluttered with numerous words alongside, obliterating their subtle essence, they will fail to participate in the reality they represent. Also, they will struggle to do their work in a congregation kept ignorant of the ecclesial history and stories from which they spring. If these situations exist, all that is achieved is ornamentation.

The line between sign and symbol in the context of liturgical space is blurred in our time. A sign points to that which it signifies. The potentially blinding and brightly illuminating character of a symbol is reduced by its presentation as a sign. A superficial and therefore shallow presentation of a symbol truncates its capacity to communicate with depth. For instance, through design techniques of transparency, a nuanced multivalent disclosure takes congregants to the threshold of mystery. The presentation of a symbol in this manner is not about new content for its own sake. Rather it references tradition, connects to community, and yields itself suggestively and mysteriously. Such visual syntax yields a language spoken to the soul.

A task of the contemporary artist who is wooed to the church as context is to clothe meaningful symbols in new garb. Our heritage of sacred symbols begs fresh representation. Our vast but dormant repository of visual potentiality needs reinvigoration. The liturgical environment is a place of action ripe for the in-breaking of numinous meaning. The actions themselves are symbolic. Breaking the bread, sprinkling the water, lighting a candle—much of what is done with gesture and movement resembles the reality it re-presents. Regardless of medium, symbolic presence and action sustain and renew. Grace upon grace upon grace.

Re-enchanting our symbols is the purview of the artists. For you artists who are believers, recall for the sake of example the events of Holy Week. They will cascade through your mind as

images. Imagine mentally casting them about in sacred space and then designing and installing them in refined symbolic guise, where they will arrest attention meaningfully.

Picture the Holy Week story in visual detail couched in narrative abstraction or fresh symbolic representation: palms representing the welcoming, grapes and wheat representing the Last Supper, a hand over a foot representing the washing of the disciples' feet, a crowing cock representing Peter's denial, coins of silver tumbling from a money bag representing Judas's betrayal, three crosses representing Calvary, and a Jerusalem cross representing Jesus's wounds. Imagine these narrative moments cloaked in a mysterious alchemy of line, shape, value, color, and texture. Take them, and give them fresh visualization unique to your means of expression.

This repertoire of image-making references bears symbolic testimony of God's reconciling act. Viewing all of these images simultaneously or additively through Holy Week offers the worshiping community the capacity for continuous movement of thought between times, between remembrance of the past for enablement of the present and empowerment of the future. Viewing all of these symbols simultaneously offers the worshiping community the opportunity to experience and appropriate as a member of the Body of Christ the whole story of God in Christ reconciling the world to God's self.

Today, there is a proliferation of congregations with highly unique and individual visual expressions for Lent, due in part to the abundance of accessible visually stimulating narrative. Vestments, from stoles to chasubles, may reinforce the visual motifs already in evidence in the paraments (pulpit, lectern, ambo, table and altar frontals).[42] When the latter are unique, conforming to the visual characteristics of the furniture and space, they speak more imaginatively than the visually predictable, sometimes banal, oftentimes symbol as sign offerings found in liturgical catalogues. Furthermore, the distance or multiple distances from which they will be seen, legislate the degree to which their symbolic content is given visual definition.

Other visually symbolic means such as stationary or processional banners (or comparable visual additions), draping the cross, and stripping the sanctuary of decorative accoutrements support the stark slash of ash crossing the foreheads of believers at Lent's start. The blotting out of light during aspects of Holy Week or the sign acts of the celebrant giving communion gesture this liturgical season symbolically. Other liturgical seasons, some of which have less overt narrative, nevertheless offer just as compelling thematic material for visual amplification.

Despite commonplace visual symbolic gestures, there is no living tradition of liturgical art. There will be no living tradition until the reclamation of symbol, critical to its reemergence.

---

42. Ambo: a raised desk similar to a lectern from which the scriptures are read and the sermon is given.
   Frontal: a movable cover or hanging for the front of an altar, table, pulpit, lectern, or ambo.

Then imaged symbols with songs joined to story will awaken souls and mediate that marvel of insight, revelation. In addition, in an environment in which handwrought works inclusive of symbols reside, there is symbolic presence testifying that creation is reverenced as a primary gospel value.

Shortly after I began accepting ecclesial commissions, a surprising experience regarding symbol occurred. It caused me to reflect deeply upon the significance of symbol in the context of a particular setting. A Roman Catholic church bearing the name of The Church of the Good Shepherd asked me to create a large work (eventually 22' in length) for their narthex. The committee in charge clearly conveyed to me that the community expected an image of the Good Shepherd in their entrance. This church resides in the lush Virginia countryside, yet most of its parishioners work in urban Washington, DC, I took no note of the latter fact when I went to work on the design.

When my solution for the space was showable in full color format and reduced scale, I met with the committee. At first, its members seemed pleased, commending the design. Slowly, however, quizzical expressions eclipsed joyful ones. Eventually, one member questioned the necessity of the sheep in the design as a visual means of explicating the idea. "What relevance do they have for us?" she asked.

My design was abstract, somewhat unrelated to traditional images of the Good Shepherd. I had faced the fact, while working in my studio, that the wall against which my work would hang was horizontal in axis rather than vertical. Since I pictured the Good Shepherd as vertical, how in the world was I going to fill the space side to side? My solution rested in resorting to the use of some traditional subject matter (sheep) in a non-traditional way.

We came to the insight together that this highly educated and biblically literate community desired a fresh approach to image-making. My approach could eschew known visual references in the Good Shepherd story. I willingly returned to the drawing board. Of course, the solution exacted twice as much work.[43]

---

43. The work is pictured on the DVD in chapter 2, "Transforming Other Ecclesial Space."

As of this writing, I am working in another church named the Church of the Good Shepherd. This one is an Episcopal Church. This time the format is a 7'circle, cast high in the church's very contemporary space over the inside entrance of its sanctuary. It is an urban church, fronting a four-lane highway. Its membership would be quite comfortable with a relatively conventional Good Shepherd image, its committee members supportive of a solution yielding such content. I have pressed the community to think differently.[44]

_____

44. The design conceived and accepted is pictured on the DVD in chapter 7, "Designs of Works in Progress."

Should creating a Good Shepherd image for a downtown church in an East Coast American city be different implicitly from one created for a church, for instance, in the southern island of New Zealand where sheep outnumber people approximately twenty to one (all other things being equal)? The answer is mediated through the mix of location, biblical literacy of the congregation, and artist.

Scripture is replete with pictorial images referencing the Good Shepherd. Psalm 23 comes immediately to mind. "The LORD is my Shepherd, I shall not want; he makes me lie down in green pastures..."[45] John 10 tells readers that Jesus is the Shepherd who will die for his flock unlike the hired hand who will run when the wolf comes. Earlier in John's chapter, the gate of the sheep-pen symbolizes Jesus, who provides the way into lasting life. John 1:29 refers to Jesus as the Lamb of God. Over and over, we are given images that reference the schema of shepherd, sheep, and lamb through which we conjure up the Christ of faith.

Placing a material conceptualization of the Good Shepherd of any ilk in ecclesial space automatically turns the image into a symbol. Freighted with extra meaning-making possibility, it participates in the multiple references it represents.

In the lamb's concreteness, you see at once an ordinary animal, a gentle animal, and the possibility of food for the human family. In its symbolic guise, the lamb is at once the carpenter in first-century Palestine, the crucified Jesus, and the paschal lamb sacrificed for our sustenance and recognized at the communion rail. In essence, the experience of seeing a representational image of the Good Shepherd ensconced in urban ecclesial locations today symbolizes the way in which the historical Jesus revealed the Christ of faith. It appeals to the piety of the believer, being devotional in character. Such an image is doing what it is supposed to do. Might we expect more?

The mitigating factor finally is the artist, who creates on the continuum, bridging pietistic purpose and fresh disclosure. The former portrays the Good Shepherd as a familiar iconic form symbolizing God's initiative in our world. The latter portrays a

---

45. See Psalm 23:1–2.

Good Shepherd who jolts the believer beyond the obvious and already familiar into a momentary startling recognition of Love given a human face. This Good Shepherd could be imagined as a figure cloaked in contemporary garb, with a different companion (a body beaten down by war, disease, poverty, etc.) the two figures crouched and interlocked abstractly, with body parts exaggerated (arms, hands, eyes). A criss-crossing and interlocking bold use of line might at once outline and run independent of the figures.

If the congregation prides itself in biblical literacy, it does not need the lamb or sheep visualized to make the leap into symbolic thought processing. An analogous image of unconditional caring is adequate. This fact reaffirms the significance of context. The image, placed as it is in a church rather than a shopping mall, will evoke simultaneous meanings in a mirage of remembrance. Scriptural texts, God's enduring embrace, and love of the other conjoin in the mental leap enacted by looking at a non-traditional image such as the one just described.

When an artist has a personal experience of the Christ of faith, he or she plumbs a deep reservoir from which to draw interpretive ideas. Several years ago a student, Maxwell Lawton, was hospitalized deathly ill. Diagnosed with AIDS, Maxwell's doctors gave him three months to live. Resolute despite ebbing strength, Maxwell insisted that his nurses disconnect his I.V. drips, enabling him to attend class on a day pass at our nearby seminary. Hours later, spent, he would reconnect.

Maxwell survived his death sentence and returned to seminary doggedly determined. For the next year and a half, he studied, watched his friends die, and coped with End-Stage AIDS. The enormity of his catastrophe overtook him in a solitary moment in his dorm room. Grief shook him to his core, consolable only as dawning awareness of Isaiah 53, a circulating text during this Advent time, seeped its way into his being. "He was despised and rejected by men; a man of sorrows, and acquainted with grief..."[46] Suddenly, Maxwell knew himself known and not alone.

---

46. Isaiah 53:3.

76

A trained artist, Maxwell had found comfort and healing, he claims, working in the far corner of the seminary arts studio. There he started to paint what he was experiencing because he knew God's grief. Under his hand, a 36" by 42" canvas titled *Man of Sorrows: Christ with AIDS* sprung to life.[47] Maxwell's Jesus, with a body racked by Kaposi's sarcoma lesions and tethered to an I.V. bottle and oxygen tank, wore a crown of thorns. Blanketed in a wash of subtly superimposed text from Matthew 25: "I was hungry…I was naked…I was sick…as you did it to one of the least of these…you did it to me," his Jesus challenged anyone willing to confront it. Maxwell's canvas talked back to the loud and shrill voices claiming that AIDS was a consequence of God's judgment upon those who deserved it.

Several years later, following repeated hospitalizations and countless drug interventions, Maxwell set off for Cape Town, South Africa. He went as a high-risk patient on an experimental oral medication to stave off impending blindness (CMV retinitis), a complication of AIDS. Ensconced in the back of St. George's Anglican Cathedral for the month of December in 1994, Maxwell inaugurated AIDS awareness month at his easel with paints, pallet, and brushes. His second and larger 4' by 6' *Man of Sorrows* sprang to life. It too was blanketed with superimposed text from Matthew 25, this time in Xhosa, Afrikaans, and English, the three languages spoken in Cape Town.

Uproar. A gathering momentum of people stormed the cathedral and demanded the painting's removal. Members of the majority population, decimated by the disease, rejoiced in Maxwell's Jesus. While his adversaries spit on him and yelled at him, others cried in the presence of the painting. They thanked him and gave him gifts, sometimes with the whisper, "Don't recognize me in the street." The stigma of AIDS crucified. Cafes buzzed. Radio commentators chattered. When Maxwell's life was threatened, he was put under cathedral custody. Newspaper reporters and television commentators companioned the crowds circling the cathedral.

---

47. To view this painting, go to the website
http://www.theotherside.org/archive/may-jun00/index.html (accessed on November 14, 2005).

The cathedral's board of trustees convened. They could not agree as to where to place the painting. Archbishop Desmond Tutu was recruited. He stepped up and agreed that the painting should be moved, moved to an empty, unused eye-level niche in the cathedral's north transept. There, before a table set with candles, pilgrims lined up to pay homage. Facing *The Man of Sorrows* was a sculpture of a black Madonna and Child, perched on a pedestal. The next day, December 21, 1994, newspapers across South Africa pealed the event. "Tutu's Yes to AIDS' Painting" read the article's caption in Durban's *The Daily News*, the city's largest daily newspaper.

Hayden Proud, curator of painting and sculpture, South African National Gallery, Cape Town, wrote the following editorial. In large bold-face caption, it bore the title: **"Christ with AIDS Painting Justified and in Line with Artistic Precedent."**

> An image of Jesus Christ suffering from Aids painted by visiting artist Maxwell Lawton has generated commentary in your column that is largely mindless, uninformed, biased and ahistorical.
>
> Mr. Lawton has provided local amateur theologians and self-appointed "art experts" with much to think about concerning the interface of AIDS and Christianity. It is a pity that the level of debate in this city should be so low, ranging from death threats made against the artist and openly declared intentions to destroy the canvas to the sanctimonious cant that has appeared in the Press. So much for the ideal of tolerance in the new South Africa.
>
> Isaiah prophesied Christ's suffering as follows…"the crowds were appalled on seeing him—so disfigured did he look—that he seemed no longer human…without beauty, no looks to attract our eyes, a being despised and rejected by men, a man of sorrows and familiar with suffering, a man to make people screen their faces; he was despised and we

78

took no account of him…we thought of him as someone punished, struck by God and brought low…they gave him a grave with the wicked…but on him lies a punishment that brings us peace, and through his wounds we are healed." (52:13–53:12)

During the Black Death of the 1300s in Germany, wooden "plague" crucifixes were carved which accentuated and emphasized Christ's horrifying suffering in terms of his human incarnation and his human flesh. In 1510, at Isenheim, the Anthonite order of hospital monks, which was solely devoted to the physical and spiritual care of those dying from an infectious gangrenous disorder, commissioned an altarpiece for their church from the painter Matthias Grünewald (1460–1528).

Its central subject was the Crucifixion. Grünewald rendered the body of Christ with harrowing attention to detail and added to it the same symptoms of disease, the lesions of Christ's suffering humanity on earth. This altarpiece [is] one of the greatest achievements of late medieval art. It is an eloquent theological exposition on the mortality of Christ's human flesh and, in another panel, of its transfigured resurrection from the grave.

Today the mystical Body of Christ, his Church, is similarly affected by a new scourge, a new incurable infection and a new fear. This is HIV infection and AIDS. If a single member of Christ's mystical body—a single Christian—is infected it affects the whole, for all are vulnerable and all are members of this body. Implicit, therefore, is the notion of Christ's body having AIDS. Mr. Lawton's concept of Christ with AIDS is not only in line with artistic precedent, but can be justified in terms of the metaphorical references to Christ's Body which abound in Scripture.

Christians are called to love, hold, embrace and support, as brothers and sisters in Christ, all men, women and children who bear in their bodies this further mark of our fallenness. As Christ comforted the sick and dying, so too must they if they are to aspire to the condition of his risen body, freed from the curse of disease and death.[48]

Shepherding Maxwell has occurred in the context of years of work embedded in the religious community. I have wrestled with this community's questions spun out, and discoursed with its disciplines in the seminary context. Artists ought to plumb the community's material, as do Maxwell and myself. Having a source text (Hebrew Bible and New Testament), the religious community draws upon a body of written material given in poetic and literary form that traverses the vast territory of human behaviors. Besides being a source of truth, inspiration, and comfort, biblical text shimmers with stories in which stricken, treacherous, naïve, saintly, and laughable characters ring with recognition. Multidimensionality, in a word. Plenty of material abounds for the artist to work with and against. Plenty of opportunity exists for the artist to work interactively with personal experience.

This way of working has its own rewards. I have integrated my personal experience and skill with the goals of the religious community and found it thoroughly rewarding. Of course, since I choose to work in their communities with a shared viewpoint, the church deals more easily with me, but not without a few skirmishes too. A church trying to renew or resuscitate itself must not ignore the artist, believer or not, in its quest to come back to life. In fact, it is in the church's best interest, renewing itself or not, to invite the arts in, difficulties or not.

A most appealing aspect of working liturgically is an encounter with symbols. In particular, I delight in engaging thoughts of

---

48. *The Cape Argus,* "Christ with AIDS Painting Justified and in Line with Artistic Precedent." January 25, 1995.

multi-layered possibilities. Once I actually design in material form the multi-layered imagery conjured up, I encapsulate the multivalent character of symbolic disclosure. By placing a transparent image from text or narrative tradition on top of a symbol, or vice versa, or confusing through complex layering of transparent fabric which piece is on top of the other, the viewer is invited, if not forced, to see beyond the symbol's concreteness. This represents one significant way in which an artist and a congregation connect.

A painter achieves transparency, that is, the ability to see through one object into another, by altering the hue (red, yellow, blue, etc.), value, or texture of the overlapping parts of the two objects. Transparency can be achieved by using fabrics as well. One way to achieve transparency is by cutting out one object (it might be a symbol) in fine net and stitching it on top of parts of two other shapes defining objects. More often than not, the use of multiple layers of netting in concert with opaque materials not only creates transparency but also creates complexity for the sake of multivalent disclosure.

The symbolic process is unique; a concrete material image opens the mind to matters spiritual. For those churches grounded in the liturgical year, the symbolic process is cogent. Its manifestations should be evident, in abundance.

The church must create a culture of hospitable affirmation for the artist and apportion an annual expenditure for aesthetic works and experiences. If the church believes that food for the soul is digested through aesthetic sustenance, then it must appropriate means for artistic endeavors. This initiative lies alongside initiatives to fund works of social justice. In fact, a congregation enthralled and captivated by the heightened awareness the arts evoke will in turn be inclined to give abundantly to a spectrum of initiatives.

The Metropolitan Memorial United Methodist Church in Washington, DC, is a case in point. When this church decided to dry clean its dusty, thirty-year-old 10' by 25' luxurious red velvet dossal cloth hanging above its high altar, it learned the cloth would disintegrate in the process. Consequently, the church chose to investigate other options, finally deciding on an iconic solution

rather than a non-iconic replacement (image-bearing work rather than a plain or patterned cloth). This decision necessitated the bringing in of artists, and each proposed a different solution. I was commissioned to cover the 250 square foot surface with painted wood tracery housing a tapestry needlepointed by members of the congregation.

Necessity (ongoing rippling requirements of the challenge) along with energizing momentum brought many volunteers

on board. Enthusiasm was infectious. Interest and involvement grew exponentially. By the time of the tapestry's installation, more financial support than the amount needed to pay for the work had been raised.

Once I completed the design work and turned over full-scale patterns and color codes, the community engaged with symbolic content in the tapestry long before its installation. On some Sundays, the bulletin contained an insert yielding a line

drawing and description of a symbolic section of the tapestry in process. On occasional Sundays following worship, children added a stitch under the supervision of the fifty plus stitchers who brought their panels of varying sizes to the church. Thus those present became acquainted with the tapestry's symbolic intentions through this process. Energized by the complexity of the fabrication process, many people unexpectedly were swept into the orbit of the gathering momentum. Consequently, after its installation, the tapestry became the new symbol around which the community gathered. Stories of its birthing, its making, its installing, and its speaking still linger.[49]

There is virtue in keeping alive threads of the tradition in new ways. The challenge for those using digital technology in their worship space is to reckon with the how of this statement. The solution is not to divest sanctuary space of symbolic representation as has been done in a few mega-churches. In an attempt to evangelize the unchurched, these churches attract new members with state of the art technology: high tech amplification, screens that appear with the flick of a switch, projections of rapidly changing images in simultaneity, dramatic lighting sources at a fingertip, etc. By stripping the sanctuary of symbolic images, an insider/outsider mentality based on those who comprehend the images and those who do not is eliminated. A sanctuary shimmering with slick technology supports performance rather than participation. It may lure but will it sustain? It is naïve to think that a church without images is not an image. This is a symbolic statement in its own way.

Churches caught up in the movement of alternative worship styles must consider the artist as an ally. The artist is the one who understands improvisation and improvises in the truest sense of the word. Improvisation honors and maintains symbolic evidences of the tradition while simultaneously creating anew. Jettisoning what was is a stopgap measure, but it is not the way for lasting sustainability.

For some artists, working in addition to or from within the religious community could be a viable and rewarding coun-

---

49. This needlepoint tapestry is the second work pictured on the DVD in chapter 1, "Transforming Liturgical Space."

terpoint to working within the triad of curators, dealers, and collectors. This triad drives an alignment between art and commerce that values trends and money and market affirmation. Art has its own priesthood who pontificate from on high. An artist succeeds in this context when its promoters and dictators of taste are supported by the correctly-informed, art-savvy rich. This system anoints the artist who succeeds. It is a tough and narrow path to follow, demoralizing for those who find it harsh and unrewarding, and perceive or seek no alternatives. Some of the work that succeeds is vapid, trendy, rewarded for its high shock-value, and heralded for its originality, albeit of questionable relevancy. Of course, the system also identifies and supports worthy artists.

Art Basel is a case in point. It not only illustrates the system described, but it also shows that symbolic representation is alive and well. Art Basel is the world's largest art spectacle. In a worldwide market with an estimated turnover of 20 billion dollars annually, Art Basel's 275 modern and contemporary art dealers woo 50,000 curators and collectors. In 2005, frenetic buyers once again charged packed booths to purchase star quality artist's work. This time, a bar of soap touted as art reportedly sold for $18,000. Displayed on a square of black velvet, this bar of soap reigned symbolically.

Made from Italian Prime Minister Silvio Berlusconi's fat removed during liposuction and confiscated by a clinic's employee, the bar of soap expressed the artist's opinion of the prime minister's politics and the artist's opposition to corruption. It bore the title of *Clean Hands*.

> The avariciousness of buyers and the bidding up of works of art is happening in quite a bizarre way said Bruce Wolmar, editor of Art and Auction magazine…"not only do they buy for pleasure, they buy for Status"…

> For Hans Ulrich Obrist, curator at the Museum of Modern Art in Paris, it is this very frisson that can be energizing. "Great artists always lead us to extraordinary experiences,

and I think that is still what we always have to look for, and it is still happening," said Obrist.[50]

Hosts of artists are ensnared by the system of support described. Some find it disagreeable and barely adequate, and others simply do not want to participate in it. While the suggestion may appear preposterous considering the distance between today's artists and the church, nevertheless I advocate an alliance. I have witnessed over and over again how artists, believers or not, have benefited from lively theological discourse and debate. Its consequences, evident in their works, tell me that informed artists can carry traditions forward symbolically in richly innovative ways. A climate of cooperation and mutual respect between artists and the church would benefit both. Lurking is the possibility of a repertoire of strikingly new, sustaining, and prophetically challenging art forms springing from our technological culture. Projected images derived from saccharine and sentimental photographs of landscapes, clip art, and a hodge-podge of differently styled lines of text would be ameliorated by an innovative artist on a large church staff (or broader governing body of the church) whose informed designs are born out of technology with originality and continuity.

The possibilities are endless. Remember, the human family has created works of art ever since it became conscious of itself. Who knew that florescent colored tubular shop lights from the Home Depot could be seen symbolically? One student filled vertical parallel gaps in his church tower with lit parallel tubes changing color with each liturgical season.[51] The three elongated narrow openings in each of the tower's four sides, now illuminated, bear symbolic witness. The openings always have, but now in a new way consistent with our age.

---

50. *USA Today*, June 19, 2005, "Bar of Soap Sells for $18,000 at Frenzied Art Basel."
51. Matt Lyons is a first-year Masters of Divinity student at Wesley Theological Seminary serving as an artist-in-residence in his church.

CHAPTER SIX

Evoking the Creative Process

S cripture is clear. It tells us we are created in the image of God, the Imago Dei.[52] What kind of image, we wonder. Maybe like a symbol. Maybe like a shadow. Maybe like a reflection. Star stuff?

The Word asserts God as creator. Did God call God's self into being? Scripture commences with God calling the world into being, and in successive acts, all that lives in it. Day one, day two, day three, day four…and we say, "How great are your works, O Lord!"[53]

Consequently, we, the children of God, bearers of the divine image, are endowed genetically with a capacity to create and to respond creatively. In what circumstances and with what frequency we do is an individual affair. Do not think of this capacity as giftedness, given to a few. Existing in abundance, it is the cheapest commodity in the world. Like all endowments given freely from our Maker, it is a gift. Sadly, this capacity can be neglected, misunderstood, stifled, and corroded beyond recognition by ignorance, poverty, and abuse. Some of the most creative expressions of human endeavor are evil. Remember that the capacity is neutral. Hitler wanted to go to art school but was denied entrance.[54] Would his imagination have been diverted? Maybe, maybe not.

---

52. Imago Dei: Latin for "image of God."
53. Psalm 92:5 (NRSV).
54. *The New Encyclopaedia, Volume 20, Macropaedia, Knowledge in Depth,* 15th Edition, "Hitler", (Chicago: Encyclopaedia Britannica, Inc., 1994) 624.

Evil always is. Its overt manifestations in the world are rampant; our unremitting proclivity for sin legendary. Like a river running through, we insist on insidiously disruptive behavior, which can be extremely creative. Its tributaries run like veins through our creatureliness. Once, through the most unlikely artistic endeavor, I experienced our startling propensity for hurtful, alienating behavior. In releasing my work, the polar reactions to it revealed the bell-shaped curve of possible creative human response.

It was April 1993. I stood at the podium before a crowd gathered for a symposium titled "Crossed Cultures." Convened to consider the tensions between the church and modern culture, it was sponsored jointly by the Yale University Institute of Sacred Music and the National Council of Churches' Department of Worship and the Arts. Commissioned to create a work for this event, my 12' 6" by 8' *Frayed Christ* resided behind me, ensconced in the pristine elegance of Yale's Marquand Chapel. Its tortured and ravaged black body inundated with pulled threads, frayed edges, and white stitching symbolized the racial strife tearing at the fabric of our existence and swirling at the foot of the hill.

I had concluded my address with the question: "Is it possible to recreate the pain of the crucifixion event independent of a cultural costume...the Christ event has been told, and I tell it once again. The story is known. Does the telling of the story make a difference? Honestly, I wonder. But I look around the world, I look down your street. God must be weeping. That is why I did this work. I know God is weeping. So I will keep telling the story in line, shape, value, color, and texture." Trailing off, this last utterance caught in my throat.

The convener asked for questions. Immediately a hand shot skyward from the back, and a gentleman jumped to his feet. This senior faculty member of the divinity school thundered a comment and question from the depth of his being. In effect, he berated me for creating a negative piece with resurrection missing. In an instant, the hushed audience and I, brought to our knees by my reading portions of Countee Cullen's poem "Black Christ" (which inspired my *Frayed Christ*), were robbed

of our participation in the sorrow of God. Derailed and disappointed, I stammered and floundered, foolishly off-center. The session ended.[55]

Letters arrived after this event. None of these letters affirmed the professor's point of view. From Yale's Institute, this came:

> I have been wanting to share with you a powerful and moving reaction to your tapestry, *Frayed Christ*, which I was privileged to witness…the tapestry was scheduled to be relo-

---

55. The singular image of the *Black Christ* was created in 1978. I chose to keep it despite opportunities for its sale generated by the differing venues in which it was shown. I knew why I chose to keep it after the commission that led to *Frayed Christ*. Countee Cullen's poem had not finished its work on me; my *Black Christ* became subsumed in *Frayed Christ*. This work can be seen on the DVD in chapter 2, "Transforming Other Ecclesial Space."

cated...when the movers entered the chapel,
their spontaneous response to the tapestry was
extraordinary. They identified immediately
with the characters represented and with the
black Christ. The careful, almost reverent way
in which they slowly carried *Frayed Christ* to
Porter Hall symbolized for me not only the
Way of the Cross, but also the sense of community that must have prevailed in the buildings of the great medieval cathedrals.[56]

Four months later, a letter arrived from a Canadian pastor. It
began:

It's been some time since Yale and I've had this
letter on my mind the whole time...the
images of the hanging are still with me in vivid
detail and colour...there was a comment made
to you after your presentation that the work
did not represent the resurrection and that it
was a negative piece.... I have been in that spot
before...with the music of a composer, or with
a prayer in our Book of Common Worship.
People have said the same thing to me about
those things. This is what I now say to
them...the work we are considering has been
brought into a community of faith. It does not
exist in neutral territory...its life is meant to be
lived in community, a resurrection community... the Word of God is read in its presence... the greatness of art is experienced
when it takes its context seriously...to isolate
any work of art is to make a graven image of
it...for me, I was humbled by the pain of a
world God so deeply loves. I was challenged as
a preacher to preach a Gospel that speaks to
that pain.... I wish it hung near me.[57]

56. Quoted from a June 1, 1993 letter from Janice Fournier.
57. Quoted from an August 18, 1993 letter from Canadian pastor Diane J.
   Strickland.

He, the professor who made the comment after the lecture, knew better. We know better. Yet we persist. Our world is broken by sin. The real body of Christ is a broken body. Remembered at the rail, "The body of Christ broken for you…" Love's redeeming work was done. "You ask me how I know he lives? He lives within my heart."[58]

To love is to suffer. The vulnerability of exposure can be lethal. It's the price we must pay for a creative life.

An individual's creative process is unique. Creative process generically is not. It is an action attempting to usher in something new—a chocolate torte with a twist, a theorem, a business venture, a poem. Risking, stumbling around, improvising, living with ambiguity, being open to possibility, sweating—all are bedrock to the experience. Some of us are more comfortable than others living in the domain of the creative process. Many are acculturated out of this capacity, robbed from participation. The creative process has dominion over me; the dreaming-up and the making are infinitely more interesting than the finished work.

In *A Midsummer Night's Dream*, Shakespeare captures the aim as well as the antic quality of creative processing. Out of the mouth of Theseus comes:

> The poet's eye, in a fine frenzy rolling,
> Doth glance from heaven to earth, from earth
>   to heaven;
> And as imagination bodies forth
> The form of things unknown, the poet's pen
> Turns them into shapes, and gives to airy
>   nothing
> A local habitation and a name.[59]

Knowing how playful yet doggedly dedicated a creative life is, much of my adult life has been spent wondering what else

---

58. A line from the hymn "He Lives," written by Alfred H. Ackley, 1933.

59. William Shakespeare, *A Midsummer Night's Dream*, Act 5, found in "The Comedies, Histories, Tragedies and Poems of William Shakespeare," edited by Charles Knight, *The National Edition, Comedies, Volume 1.* London: Charles Knight, 90, Fleet Street, 1851, p. 472.

overtly creative people have in common.[60] Based on observation, I suspected they might share similar attributes but never knew what these were until one fateful evening. Hurrying into the Kennedy Center to hear a concert, I sprinted through the lobby and was startled by an enormous exhibit. Its alien presence caught my attention. Out of the corner of my eye, I caught its title: *CREATIVITY: THE HUMAN RESOURCE.* Every once in a while, we are arrested in our tracks and are never the same again. In an instant, in the scheme of things, clarity shimmered. It was a revelatory moment.

This exhibit was produced as a gift to the public by Standard Oil Company of California and its Chevron Family of Companies to mark its 100th anniversary. It inquired into the same question that had plagued me. Do creative people share attributes in common? A designated team of investigators explored the workplaces, studios, and laboratories as well as interviewed and studied the contributions of fifteen outstanding Americans to ascertain the answer. At the time of the investigation, all were alive. Each had ushered in new meaning for the human family on a colossal and groundbreaking scale, this being the defining qualification for inclusion. Each exhibited a quintessential amount of creative capacity. Each was given presence through personal, priceless, insightful materials (notebooks, sketches, diagrams, models, tapes, and films) in the interactive exhibition.

I missed the first half of the concert and instead met the following giants who have left their indelible mark on the arts and sciences: Jonas Salk, Margaret Mead, Buckminister Fuller, Romare Bearden, Charles Townes, Linus Pauling, Judy Chicago, John Cage, Melvin Calvin, Lawrence Halprin, George Nelson, Simone Ramo, Harry Hess, Roman Vishniac, and Jasper Johns. Posted on a simple plaque were the seven attributes possessed by all fifteen outstanding Americans. The plaque read as follows:

---

60. The video *Creativity: Touching the Divine* (U.S. Catholic Conference, 1994) offers an inspiring look at aspects of creative processing expressed through the lives of approximately eight people working in differing vocational contexts. All of their creative undertakings manifest a connectedness to the sacred.

Creative people:

1. Challenge assumptions

2. Take risks

3. Take advantage of chance

4. See in new ways

5. Recognize patterns

6. Make connections

7. Construct networks

No descriptive text accompanied this list. It was self-explanatory; the concepts emoted from the presentation. I hold myself accountable to these attributes of the creative capacity given to me. Following is a minimalist explication of them based upon my own experiences.

Creative people challenge assumptions. When I studied at Wesley Theological Seminary, I was dismayed by the absence of the arts (with the exception of music) in its curriculum and its member schools in the Washington Theological Consortium.[61] Upon completion of my studies in 1979, I deemed my experience of theological education truncated. Propelled by an overpowering sense that the arts should be present, I approached the dean and president together the day after I graduated and proposed an artist-in-residence position. I had a one-page statement of ideas, a few clues as to how I would implement these ideas, and passionate conviction. Initially rejected but later reconsidered following the proposal's disclosure to the full faculty, my suggestion was implemented. I was unaware at the time that asking the question, "Where are the arts?" was challenging an assumption—the assumption that theological education as delivered was adequate.

Creative people take risks. When creating, it is one thing to listen to your work, quite another to surrender to it. This capacity defines the extent to which the artist risks. Questions plague the

---

61. At that time, the Washington Theological Consortium was comprised of Episcopal, Lutheran, United Methodist, non-denominational, and Catholic seminaries and schools of theology.

risk-taking artist. What if I change that red to fuschia? What if I tone down that transitional shape, and ratchet up the contrast here? What if I intensify the edge of that line and eliminate that blue over there? Willing to confound the already satisfying synthesis of parts, the courageous artist will submit to the lurking sensibility that more "what ifs" must be tried. In these paralyzing moments, lasting for hours and even days, the artist risks change that sometimes is so radical it destroys what is.

Creative people take advantage of chance. All my adult life, I have loved the expression, attributed to Pasteur, "Chance favors only the prepared mind."[62] In other words, do your homework, thereby posturing yourself to take advantage of chance.

Creative people see in new ways. If your world is always expanding because you challenge assumptions, take risks, and take advantage of chance, then you not only see new things but also begin to look at things in new ways. The point is, the more you see, the more you begin to look to see.

Creative people recognize patterns. The more my life and my art emerge as one, the more frequently underlying patterns of connectedness between things appear. Relationships among things, activities, and chance occurrences seem to have significance. Patterns hold things together, which when recognized aid in discerning new ways of perceiving them. I intentionally acknowledge and name these patterns to aid in the process of living creatively.

Creative people make connections. Connections occur in a multiplicity of ways: connections with people, ideas, concrete things, possibilities. The list is endless. A concrete example of this occurs frequently in my studio. When I am creating a new design solution, I often use paper, cutting from it a form or a shape, and then discard the remaining. As the process progresses, I notice the rejected, thrown-away cuts, dropped on the floor or tossed into a wastebasket. Their shapes, values, and colors in their aggregate appear in a new way. Suddenly, I realize

---

62. Louis Pasteur, "Address given on the inauguration of the Faculty of Science, University of Lille," 7 December 1854; in R. Vallery-Radot, *La Vie de Pasteur* (1900), Ch. 4.

their connectedness to my work in progress. I retrieve them and use them in the design unfolding under my hands.

Creative people construct networks. This concept is understood more readily because it is valued and discussed in our market-driven society. By analogy, my small experimental tapestries rendered in the Gobelin tapestry technique picture the concept. The warp (tightly drawn vertical threads) and the weft (packed down horizontal threads woven over and under the warp threads) create an interconnected fabric structure. Because this weaving technique is pictorial, the weft threads end at different places, building upon themselves until the final one terminates the building of the shape desired, hue-, intensity-, and value-specific. Some shapes are incredibly important, others moderately so, and others supportive in their quiet presence. This pictured analogy points to the interconnected complexity of networking as well as its significantly differing consequences.

In the naming of these seven attributes shared by persons responding to a diversity of contexts and stimuli, those who saw the Standard Oil exhibit in its travels were reminded that the potential for letting loose one's own creative impulses and energies comes as birthright. New choices, new possibilities, and new meanings are unleashed for the human family when facile solutions are rejected in favor of living un-anxiously in the mystery of the knowing that one's own imaginings are reliable. Those who saw the exhibit came away with the "sense of the world as one action—if only we can see it—the sense that, as Albert Einstein insisted, 'God does not play at dice.'"[63]

Clearly, the attributes of a creative mentality trigger similar behaviors across fields of human endeavor. In terms of defining those behaviors, I turn to my own creative process to explicate them. When an artist undertakes a creative process attempting resolution of a challenge, stages, sometimes distinct, define the activity. Their edges more often blur, and the stages themselves may exist in simultaneity relative to the complexity of the challenge. These stages for me bear the names of: acquisition, frustration, incubation, illumination, articulation, and communication.

---

63. Robert Shankland, *Essay* (companion piece to the exhibition), p. 6.

The yielding to a creative response when challenged to create a work for an ecclesial space begins with the first stage, the **Stage of Acquisition**. This information-gathering stage, this stage of conscious thought, involves the looking at and naming of the disparate aspects of the challenge. The cognitive activity of this stage saturates the mind with useful information, gathered, sorted out, and categorized. The patterns, the dominant sightlines, the scale of parts, and the principle colors in the ecclesiastical space mix in my mind with memories of all I learned about the community.

Into my potpourri of information is added the known and unknown data regarding technique and craft along with thematic intentions. And finally, I ask, "How does one fit all this together?" There is a sense of unconnectedness in this stage of investigation, when the pieces lie scrambled yet simultaneously hint at the possibility of reassembly in a new configuration of meaning.

There is a deep affinity between creative processing and spirituality, if spirituality is understood as the intertwining of divinity with human experience. Particular kinds of coherences between the spiritual journey and an artist's process adhere in creation-centered spiritual traditions of medieval mysticism, Celtic spirituality, and insights gleaned from Process Theology. The medieval model of spirituality is structured on several paths of interconnected and interdependent understandings. It defines a faith journey aimed towards wise living. In the first path, creation is viewed sacramentally. It celebrates the blessings abundantly manifest in creation, affirms them, and gives thanks for them. The God of the Covenant is a God of blessing, breathing divine breath (ruach) into all creation, calling forth a response of reciprocation.[64]

The artist could say that the information-gathering stage, the **Stage of Acquisition**, is a way of reciprocal engagement, a way of joining with creation by submersion within it. For instance, artists tend to work from the particular places in which they find themselves. When recovering from serious illness in 1970, I was invited to create work simultaneously for the Lutheran church in

64. Ruach: Hebrew word for divine breath.

my neighborhood and the chapel at the National Naval Medical Center, where I was a patient. Never had I created work for a religious space. My positive interactions with the clergy from both places made me curious about their worlds. I said yes.

Later I realized that I was responding reciprocally to what was given. The completion of those solicited works made me theologically curious. That is why I went to study in the seminary. And my work as artist in the church flourished because later the seminary gave me an institutional base. Bound by where I was, I submerged and embraced. It is the artist's way.

As the weight of the challenge infuses my mind, anxiety and ambiguity arise, moving me to the second stage, the **Stage of Frustration**. Confusion is imposed because I am unable to arrive at a solution grounded only in rational, analytical, sequential, cognitive thought. I leave the studio after a day's efforts excited, but I return the next day to find the work flat. In this second stage of frustration, the pressure builds in the face of the chaos necessary and empowering to a creative response. Whether it is the idea seeking expression, or the materials of expression behaving obstinately, I am fixated upon achieving a unity of the disparate parts, a balance between warring dissimilarities.

> Seeking patterns, drawn to form and design, creative people at the same time refuse to clutch at them. Psychological tests have shown that they also love the challenge of complexity, asymmetry, and incompleteness. They turn away from the easily grasped and already completed, prefer the complicated and unfinished. This finding bears out Keats' observation about Negative Capability. They enjoy their perplexities, live un-anxiously with confusion, because they seem content to wait patiently for an ordering of their own to occur to them.[65]

Some confuse the frustration, chaos, and ambiguity inherent in this stage for burnout, and terminate the process. I have learned

---

65. Shankland, Essay, pp. 7–8.

to reside in this place and even honor it. For me the notion of a creative principle, the God of blessing, is at work in the world. Therefore, I let go and thrash about, trying to incubate a solution. This requires radical trust in the process, not a terribly difficult mindset for an artist who learns from spiritual traditions that a reliable faith can be built upon trust in the creative manifestations of an incarnate God. Think of the promises of the parables, iconic to the Christ of faith and the Jesus of history. I believe that an insight, a solution, will come. We know that the great gift of life is that it forever reverberates with new possibilities. Sometimes the solution takes hours, sometimes days, sometimes weeks, and sometimes months. But it will come. Meanwhile, I live uneasy, postponing gratification.

Unfortunately, I get in the way of a solution. When a deadline is impending and I cannot make what I am doing work, I press on, imposing and controlling. Spiritual traditions teach the wisdom of letting go, of emptying, of facing the dark night of the soul as a catalyst for new creation or spiritual maturity. I busy myself because I cannot face nothingness. While I know by analogy that the seed sinks into the ground to sprout, I resist this essential experience.

> Do you think it is easy to change?
> Ah, it is very hard to change and be
>   different.
> It means passing through the waters of
>   oblivion.[66]

In the third stage of the creative process, the **Stage of Incubation**, the percolating imagination has taken over and presides. Often outside the realm of conscious awareness, frequently at the level of the subconscious or unconscious state of sleeping and dreaming, all gathered information freely floats. A dawning awareness of the unique alchemy brewing in the two hemispheres of the brain grips the artist. The right hemisphere, the seat according to today's science of the relational, circuitous, intuitive, and simultaneous capacities of the mind for looking

66. D. H. Lawrence, *The Complete Works of D. H. Lawrence* (New York: 1971), p. 727. This poem is titled "Change."

at complexity, gnaws on the information gathered by the left hemisphere's capacity for objective, successive, sequential, linear, and propositional input made in the first stage, that of acquisition. The cognitive shift from left to right hemisphere enables the mind to see large amounts of information simultaneously, picturing things and ideas in volumetric configuration. This resembles the filling up of a three-dimensional sphere rather than a stretching out of a sequential ordering onto a straight line. Thus, the imagination can play with the fitting together of seemingly disparate parts. New orientations percolate. The obvious falls away to begin revealing the hidden in this stage of incubating ideas.

The brooding strife wrought by these stages is tinged with psychic pain, causing me to reflect upon its place in the spiritual journey. Some traditions teach that the soul grows by subtraction. Only by bearing the burden of pain thoroughly does one move through it, beyond it. Work is forged; soul is forged.

This synthesizing function and gestating activity advances the creative response to its next possibility. By allowing the **Stage of Incubation** to have its reign, the fourth stage, the **Stage of Illumination,** dawns. It yields the insight that elevates all of what is transpiring into the possibility of becoming. Here a glimpse of refracted meaning from the whole breaks into conscious thought. The idea is born; the new is born. The spirit of God is with me in this moment of intrusive insight. Faith recognizes this moment of creative breakthrough as the in-breaking of the Divine. It is a grace filled moment, and it is a gift given in the collaborative effort of my own becoming. The spark of divinity within ignites, and I carry on the reciprocal ongoingness of creation. This moment is born by yielding to the polar opposites of submersion through embrace and subtraction through letting go. The creative stages, steps, or passages that negotiate these opposites, by whatever name, empower the building of our worlds.

Found in the essay companioning the Standard Oil exhibition, Shankland says:

> The Nobel physicist Charles Townes views science as part of religion, both connected with the emotional experience of revelation.

He had one of his own revelations one Sunday morning in Franklin Park, Washington. Frustrated in solving a huge problem on which he and others had worked long and hard, he sits on a bench among the azaleas, "and there in the spring morning enjoyed the freshness and beauty of these gay flowers, musing over why we had so far failed. The moment of insight was no more vivid and complete than any other in my experience. Suddenly I recognized the fallacy in my previous thinking and that of others. A three-minute calculation on the back of an envelope showed that such a system could be built."[67]

67. Shankland, *Essay*, p. 5.

This time of in-breaking insights sets into motion the next stage of the creative process, the **Stage of Articulation**. Whether the insight takes shape from the hands of the artist, the calculations of a scientist, or the mouth of the preacher, this next stage of the process is freighted with procedure, sometimes frenzied. The assembly of fragments of thought and fact for the preacher, for instance, are reassembled in this fifth stage, empowered by the intrusive insights from the previous stage. The outline gives way to full-blown sentences, which in turn shape paragraphs, directing light towards visibility of the whole. Like the potter, the preacher by analogy not only pushes the clay but also is pushed by it. The erasure of this word or that to make way for another parallels the artist's process of correction and change called "pentimento." A new direction to the movement of painted arm or hand, a different inclination of the head, or the flat out painting over and thus erasure of one object to make way for another are evidences of a change of mind, or should I say, evidences of the working mind. The first thought is replaced by the second, and then by the third, in this repenting of the mind, which is a reflection of the way the imagination sees with simultaneity.

This making of thought visible and consumable by the artist and preacher begs selection and magnification of detail. Whether it means adjectives modifying a noun or raising the intensity of a hue on the canvas, the process of elaboration brings the work of both to sight and focus. The process at this point in this **Stage of Articulation** is heroic, for it demands a doing and being of oneness, an obedient surrender to the materials that claimed their passions and to which their imaginations yielded. In the doing, the being emerges in such particularity with paint or biblical text that the product of the particularity may open a window on archetypal experience.

For the preacher working towards a Sunday deadline and for the artist working towards an installation date, this stage reminds us of the time-bounded nature of many processes. Certainly it is a time of perspiration. Without hard work, the creative impulse lies fallow. Despite the reality of a time frame, stages of the creative process live by their own necessity. It is an act of faith to live in the mystery of the unknowable and wait upon the quickening of the imagination to set into motion resolutions obliterating chaos and ambiguity.

In the creation-centered traditions, the pivotal point of the Christian story teaches that the creator of life overwhelmed death at the cross to serve the purposes of living. Love energized a triumph. The outcome of full submission to submersion and subtraction empowers us to imaginatively carry on the ongoingness of creation. And when our imaginations, forged by the previous paths, fuel compassionate acts, wise living is achieved. Love, the driving energy behind such acts, arrives again. A moment of justice is wrought in the world.

> What does the LORD require of you but to do
> justice, and to love kindness, and to walk
> humbly with your God? [68]

---

68. Micah 6:8 (NRSV).

When installed, my work advances my creative process into its last stage, the **Stage of Communication**. I relinquish it to community seemingly clothed in complexity, like a sermon that hangs in the air not because it communicates in the fashion of "this is what I mean," but rather because it lives through the power of suggestion and nuance, obliquely. Both initiate creative thoughts from the other. The artful sermon and the artwork are invitations to meaning-making.

The creative response unleashed in the listener by such proclamation from the pulpit or visual emanation from the wall sow a sacred journeying together. Curiously, after my work arrives in community, I learn of meaning evoked from it that was initially concealed from me. I have discovered that my finished and unleashed work has a life of its own, speaking to people in ways never imagined. I also suspect, having recognized parallels between spiritual journeying and my creative processing, that spiritual growth, like artistic growth, is perfected by practice.

Some say an artist's work is a metaphor for living. Through my unique process, I gather up the stresses and strains of daily life and recast them metaphorically in the created order of my work. As each new studio challenge imposes a plethora of unresolved issues in tandem with the tensions of the day, this cyclical process propels me from restless agitation, off-centeredness, and estrangement back to the core and ground of my being. In its dark moments, there is doubt and lack of trust that insights and solutions will come. When I have passed to the other side of the yawning and sometimes gaping abyss made starkly real by an approaching deadline or impasse while creating a work, I am aware once again that I am the recipient of a gift divinely given.

As the crowning glory of creation, we have the capacity to create because we are a reflection of our Creator. This extraordinary capacity denied to the rest of our animated world means we bring into existence something that did not exist before, and that something brings new value and new meaning to the human situation. This gift of creative potential is the human resource with which we all build our world. Through this creative cycle I am restored to deep faith. It is in the experience of doing my work that I am brought back to the tenets of the

Church's teaching. It is not the other way around. The extraordinary fact is that the sanctity of this restorative process, wherein the Spirit of God breaks in, conspires to make me want to, in the final words of Charles Wesley's hymn, "cast [my] crowns before thee, lost in wonder, love, and praise."[69]

As I have said, much of present-day art is seen in the intermediary context of the gallery. However, within the aggregate of human experience, much art emerged as sight-specific work shaped by its context and permanent to it. This relatively outmoded way of working is still legitimate. My artwork, empowered by community, is by definition contextual. Because we are, I am. I have no problems with the notion of service, or servanthood, because I do not think it means the loss of my autonomy. It is an opportunity to learn, grow, and indeed be transformed myself. My work is always my best offering. In Christian community, we aid in each other's becoming.

Like Jacob, we must wrestle with the angels, risking the agony and the ecstasy of living into the fullness of our potential. We are intended to be initiating centers of life, contributing to the gracious work of transformation. Creation bears the imprint of God.

---

69. Charles Wesley, "Love Divine, All Loves Excelling," 1747.

CHAPTER SEVEN

Engaging in Participatory Aesthetics

W hen an ecclesial community contemplates acquiring art, it is helpful to think in terms of art as product, process, and proclamation comprised of non-verbal vocabulary. The community has a choice regarding which aspect of the artistic acquisition it will emphasize. For instance, the community might choose an artist from several interviewed, ensconce him or her in a temporary church-based space and ask him or her to create the work in situ.[70] In this scenario, the process undergirding the artist's work gets attention. Or, the artist might be asked to create a finished work and install it. In this instance, the focus is entirely on the product. Ask the artist to visit several times—once during a church lecture series to discuss the body of his or her work, and then again when he or she is crafting the commissioned work to discuss its progress and complexities. These intermediate steps enlighten the community regarding the artist's intent, purpose, and expressive use of vocabulary and its syntax.

Another alternative is one wherein an artist is invited to design a work that members of the community fabricate. This is an instance of participatory aesthetics. In the experience of fabricating (painting, sewing, constructing, cutting, hammering, gluing, etc.) an already designed work, the participating members of the congregation discover why the artist made specific design choices. Gradually, they recognize the aesthetic consequences of these choices, discuss them, and pass on to the wider community the knowledge and excitement gleaned from the

---

70. In situ: in its original place; in its context.

experience. They also deduce the necessity of reciprocity in receiving meaning from a work of art.

Art as product and process cannot be overemphasized. Historically, their independent identities kept them distinct. Today, the boundary blurs. Art as process can become the product of an acquisition. The church commissions both. For those who think of art as a fixed and unchangeable product, having little or no knowledge of its undergirding process, picture an iceberg. By analogy, what you see above the surface of the water is what you know (product). The enormity of that which is not seen, the 75% below the surface, is comparable to the complexity of the time-intensive process the artist undertakes (process). What a difference it makes to see an iceberg in its entirety.

Art undertaken as process introduces challenging dynamics, especially when grafted onto critical functions of the church: worship, education, fellowship, and outreach. Imagine a potter throwing a pot on a wheel in full view while the preacher preaches on Jeremiah 18. Imagine a Lenten Sunday school classroom in which the children paint a paper carpet of Holy Week events running the length of the sanctuary's center aisle or chapel aisle. Once installed, all walk the walk.

Imagine young teenagers scribbling interpretive marks on pre-cut strips of colored fabric, evolving from their understanding of a single line in the Apostle's Creed. And each week during fellowship time, they weave strips from another line of the Creed into a preassembled wire structure that resembles the front of a house. In the structure, there is a void in the middle, indicative of a doorway. Through the weaving process, the clarity of the markings is intentionally lost, but the colors of the strips and the memories triggering the interpretive markings reverberate in the minds of those participating. When all youth have responded to each line of the creed and the woven wall with a doorway emerges, encourage all congregants to walk through it. Reciting the Creed ever after will never be the same.

Imagine inviting in the homeless and giving them materials (paint, clay, fabrics, pastels, etc.). Encourage them to create images relevant to their experiences. Honor their creations. Ask them to share their images with one another and the person(s) companioning this undertaking. They will have an experience of joyous authority, which is rare for them. Such activity may evolve into an ongoing act of hospitality. Bound collections of images, a designated space for changing their creations, or the processing of their work into the sanctuary are possible outcomes of a commitment.

Such events are vivid and precious in the context of the church. I once met a woman in a Washington, DC, church shelter who stunned me with her intelligence and astonished me with her sewing skills. To this day I am disgusted with myself because I did not provide her (the shelter) with a sewing machine, which was my initial impulse. Her way of life would have improved, and perhaps the way of life of those who followed.

What we do, we know. What is under the hands begins to speak its own language. Participants engaged in art-making processes discover how effects such as balance, movement, and repetition comprised of lines, shapes, and colors in an art work cohere. In the syntax of their mysterious alchemy, they learn that certain elements in the work dominate while others lie subordinate in order to evoke from the viewer an intended response. Something else happens too. From a Christian perspective, art-making intertwines with the Spirit at work with our gifts; we become co-creators, continuing the ongoing act of creation.

Working in tandem with a spiritual sensibility is richly meaningful. Creative and prayerful people initiate processes that strive towards a new synthesis—one a material canvas reflective of its creator, the other a spiritual canvas reflective of the Imago Dei. Artists co-create with their work in their own emergence, just as prayerful people co-create with God in their own formation.

When I engage with a community in a project of participatory aesthetics, its members discover and experience what I know. I know that my studio is sacred space. I know that art-making is a form of extrovert meditation. I know that my doing is a framework through which I work out my spiritual life. I know that the Christian doctrine of Trinity sheds light on what makes a work of art, art.

The author of Hebrews said, "He (God) has spoken to us by a Son.... He reflects the glory of God and bears the very stamp of his nature, upholding the universe by his word of power."[71] The Christ of faith imaged in first-century Palestine in the person of Jesus is God's creation for our salvation. His remembered utterances, sacred in origin and ever-present through the hovering spirit of holiness, generate God-reflective impulses and acts through others.

Image and power are the critical words in comprehending how our Trinitarian formulation undergirds the art-making process. It works this way for me. I image forth into visual format what I am responding to in thought, feeling, and imagination. I become known to myself through each work I create. I behold myself, my image, in my creation, in the incarnated material body of the sum total of my experience revealed to me through its created form. This revealing of thought, emotion, and imagination, otherwise dim until expressed through material transformed, now is made known. It is no longer dimly perceived but fully perceived, given back, and integrated into myself. My creative impulse to recast into material form that which is, fuels a process that evolves into a work, a product with power. Once the creation is unleashed into community, it has a power of its own, independent of the artist yet of the artist, to evoke from others a response.

Through the radical particularity of an artist's experience expressed, something gets said that sometimes strikes the core of our being, center to center. Occasionally, very, very occasionally, the revealing through a work of art is so shimmering, so dazzling with clarity (Vermeer's little masterpieces), that its resident power not only sustains generations but also endures for centuries as epiphanies of meaning. Whether the aggregate is named as Idea, Image, and Power; Experience, Expression, and Recognition; or some combination thereof, the consequence is a tri-part interconnectedness.

In my experience, the communities who engage in and live alongside an art-making process prosper. When a community creates a work designed by an artist, its members dig into an experience of

---

71. Hebrews 1:2–3.

participatory aesthetics. By the time their joint efforts evolve into the work of the people, members read non-verbal vocabulary, value visual proclamation, discern seasonal symbology, and develop aesthetic sensibility. They experience evocation instead of description, insight instead of illustration. Community blossoms. Community, energized and agitated by the complexity of the challenge, enlarges rather than shrinks. Lurking is the knowledge that creative undertakings expand our world.

Also lurking are amazing antidotes for bruised personalities. Once during a day-long frenzy spent transforming a space into a temporary liturgical space, one among the thirty tethered to this adventure in participatory aesthetics said, "You remind me of a book I read called *A Soprano on Her Head.*" Defensive, I wryly shot back "up and down ladders all day creating on my feet. No wonder!"

Surprisingly, a week later *A Soprano on Her Head* arrived. Reading along half-engaged, I suddenly sat upright with a start, in a state of shock. The author was commenting on a powerful encounter with the work of an Israeli artist seen in a Paris gallery. "No!" I said, "This can't be! How is this possible?" I read a few pages more until the episode ended.

The artist mentioned was an invited artist-in-residence who would soon arrive at the seminary for the coming year. The sender did not know this. The episode described was incidental to the book, and it was not as if we had invited a world-famous artist accustomed to massive press coverage. With so many competent artists in this world making choices almost unlimited, this was an astonishing coincidence. The surprise and delight ushering from this coincidence redeemed my lingering embarrassment over behaving in a frenzy.

I comfort myself with the extravagantly rich words found in the last chapters of Exodus. I suspect the artists mentioned there had also paid their dues, developing their skills in other contexts. Bezalel is called by name, and Oholiab is appointed with him. The text describes the attributes given to these artists and elucidates expectations. Scripture also calls others who work with their hands to share in the responsibility of creating worship space:

> All who are skillful among you shall come and
> make all that the LORD has commanded: the
> tabernacle, its tent and its covering, its clasps
> and its frames, its bars, its pillars, and its
> bases...the finely worked vestments for minis-
> tering in the holy place.[72]

Present-day philosophers of art posit the theory that cultural
diversity demands an art of one's own. I therefore interpret this
to mean that the church needs an art of its own. What *kind* of
art depends on the community. Some need refurbishment and
refreshment in the sanctuary chancel. Others wish to mark the
narthex with a welcoming work. Often the fellowship hall,
sometimes an abysmal basement-level hodgepodge of things,
needs visual uplift. Spiritual communities exist in tension
between what has been and what will be as the Holy Spirit animates the community in its proclamation. Change is inevitable,
but growth is optional. Participatory aesthetics provides a rich
opportunity for discovery and a potent means of growth.

The rewards reaped are beyond visualization. The art-making
process not only enriches the spiritual dimension of participants' lives but also can be a source for its emergence, formation,
and even existence. I have seen instances wherein people outside
the community are grafted into it for artistic purposes but then
linger and finally stay for spiritual nourishment. In these
moments when art becomes a means of grace, we know we are
on holy ground. Spiritual formation shackles us to the tension
of divine/human dissonance. We tug and pull while being
tugged and pulled, not unlike an art-making process.

The works of participatory aesthetics I have undertaken
require all different kinds of people skills, not the least of
which is leadership. Invariably, among the many emerges one
who resourcefully recruits, engages, and then leads the effort.
One such person, when asked to reflect on her experience as
a leader of a sanctuary project underway, wrote:

> This project is vast in scope and requires
> an equally large leap of faith for financing,

---

72. Exodus 35:10–11, 19 (NRSV).

construction, as well as the cutting and sewing of each set of panels and paraments. Could we raise the necessary funds? Could we adequately relate the design and intended impact to the congregation? Could we provide the needed hands to cut and sew the pieces? ... Often women who have taken on the task of cutting and sewing these pieces have shared their heartfelt joy in being able to use their talents and gifts to create new opportunities for visual worship.... When congregants have offered newly discovered insight into the design and its personal meaning, we feel nothing less than sheer joy.... The excitement of the worshipers is evident in their financial support to complete the project.[73]

---

73. Taken from a letter by Julie Austin concerning a sanctuary project at Westminster Presbyterian Church, Greensboro, NC, 2005. The extraordinary energy and effort given by Julie to this ongoing project is immeasurable.

Work in participatory aesthetics requires time, from a week to years, until the process yields a completed product. This way of working offers an antidote to our culture's proclivity for instant gratification. In fact, rather than echoing the mind-numbing rapidity of slick images given as daily diet, the inherently slower pace of a participatory venture in aesthetics mitigates the modern dilemma in mediating the Word through image. When a handwrought work resides, being real rather than a copy, its value rests in its relationship to materials transformed.

The church, by nature, keeps improvising its methods of proclamation as it adapts to new times. Participatory aesthetics provides one of those means of adaptation. Like most artistic efforts, this requires funding, and such funding often comes from memorial gifts. However, when memorial funds are enshrined in a work, family members of the deceased expect permanence of placement or permanence of the work itself. Thus a potential problem exists when the work is moved or yields to age.

Memorial funds are both an asset and a liability. Ecclesiastes reminds us, "For everything there is a season, and a time for every matter under heaven."[74] A gentle reminder to the family of the deceased that permanence is relative wards off problems before they arise. The following words reflect the intense emotion underwriting a memorial work. They also reflect a healthy perspective regarding a particular work's seasonal, and therefore limited, role.

> Later as I shared a time of reflection with some of the folks who made this project come to life, I thanked them for their beautiful, enduring work and for the standard of perfection they attained. Thanks to their endeavors I will forever see my mother's eyes (…the blue

74. Ecclesiastes 3:1 (NRSV).

of her eyes could be seen in the fabrics…) and feel her spirit in Westminster's sanctuary during the season of Advent.[75]

The senior pastor, reflecting on this church's ongoing sanctuary project in participatory aesthetics, wrote:

> Sensitive in their interpretation of the liturgical seasons, these artistic expressions capture the mood and message of each season and add a visual message to the worship experience. Our congregation has been particularly pleased with the seamless integration of these liturgical panels into our present worship

---

75. Taken from a reflection written by Anne Edelblut Hendrix, who contributed funds in honor of her mother to a sanctuary project at Westminster Presbyterian Church, Greensboro, NC

space: They enhance without overwhelming, augment without dominating, and tie together the different liturgical symbols of our worship space into a unified whole. Without a doubt, they are a tremendous enhancement to the life of our congregation.[76]

Upon the completion of the second set of liturgical panels at the church attended by the three persons quoted above, all who lent their hands to this endeavor celebrated, including the gentlemen who engineered the 45' platform on which the panels sit.[77] Around extra-large tables set with wonderful foods in front of a roaring fire, volunteers reminisced and shared stories. I attended and listened avidly.

Although these celebrants talked enthusiastically about tackling the project's next phase, their conversations coalesced around two themes: gratitude for the final flourish of activity making possible the meeting of Advent's deadline, and anticipation of a well-deserved and well-earned hiatus from continued activity.

A completed work makes claims on its creators. Genesis 1 says repeatedly, "And God saw that it was good." Do not disavow the notion of creative satisfaction. When we are fulfilling some aspect of what it means to be in the divine image, celebration is in order. Genesis 2:3 says, "So God blessed the seventh day and hallowed it, because on it God rested from all the work that he had done in creation." Rest lies at the very root of creativity. All cycles of life concur; winter's rest renews summer's yields. Remember the Sabbath, and keep it holy. Remember that rest nourishes the cyclical character of a creative life.

---

76. Taken from a reflection by Reverend Bob Henderson concerning a sanctuary project at Westminster Presbyterian Church, Greensboro, NC.

77. The designs and images of some of the completed works can be seen on the DVD in chapter 7, "Designs of Works in Progress."

CHAPTER EIGHT

Sponsoring Artists-in-Residence

For me, a great paradox exists. In a time when anything intended to be art is called art, and when the church as context is a relatively irrelevant part of the aesthetic equation, I am encouraging religious communities to support artists-in-residence. I am telling artists that religious communities offer a viable place in which to work. In these contexts, the artistic imagination is challenged to wrestle and/or mingle with the mystery and majesty of the Mighty One. Why not the church and the seminary? Granted, differences generated by a variety of viewpoints, theologies, and traditions manifested in denominational sensibilities might skew the choice of artist and art, but they should not prevent an alliance.

Why doesn't the church look upon the arts community as a new mission field for hospitality rather than conversion? Better the climate between the two communities for the benefit of both. Offer a hospitable overture. Contemporary models of relating, which eschew widespread evidences of models of estrangement, could be created. The model of art as the handmaiden of religion too often prevails. At its worst, this model perpetuates dead symbols and propaganda, and at its best, it offers objects of devotion, devoid of a prophetic edge. This model truncates possibility. If art bears truth from its own point of view, how can it be a handmaiden? Instead, we should foster models of mutuality.

Why not look upon the artist as a new ally in the spiritual quest? Within reach of religious communities are numerous artists who would thrive as artists-in-residence in a church and/or a seminary setting. At our seminary, a denominationally diverse faculty has welcomed and given place and space to artists seeking community, nurture, and encouragement to create works within the context of theological discourse.[78]

We have discovered that the resident artists generally celebrate, lament, or diagnose what is. Whether wandering in the wilderness or relishing what is, these artists have roamed the range of human response. By voicing our thoughts and feelings, their works speak for us with the stridency of the prophets and in the manner of the psalms of praise and lament.

Artists who celebrate what is begin by extracting a slice of life, an awareness, an observation (a simple sensibility perhaps as enchanting as the play of light across an empty room). They go to work cutting, tearing, pounding, chiseling, mixing, etc., and material is transcended. Artists who lament what is engage in a similar process, but their works sign a pathos resident in the human condition. Artists who diagnose what is create art that has revelatory power by standing at the edge of what is known, conscious of something more. Such an artist embraces the chaos of ambiguity imposed by the creative process, as well as that imposed by his or her critique of what is. Replete with imbalances, oppositions, and seeming irreconcilabilities, this artist makes sense of what is by persisting until raw material is shaped into a startling resolution. A wake-up call. A dark prophecy.

Art of this ilk may appear abrasive, literally and figuratively, and may contain colors and shapes in opposition, discordant harmonies, jagged edges. But the promise and mystery of the unexplained permeate such works. They invite others to enter into their shapes and colors, to imagine meaning, and to see new God-given possibilities otherwise not fathomed. These kinds of works belong in our spaces, both churches and seminaries. Situating artistic excellence in a theological framework, however it manifests itself, is a wise investment, literally and figuratively.

Ultimately, great work by its very nature is elastic enough to be shaped into the contours of others' experience. Frederick Buechner says it well:

---

78. Over the past twenty-five years, Wesley Theological Seminary has given residency positions to approximately sixty artists.

Rembrandt put a frame around an old woman's face. It is seamed with wrinkles. The upper lip is sunken in, the skin waxy and pale. It is not a remarkable face. You would not look twice at the old woman if you found her sitting across the aisle from you on the bus. But, it is a face so remarkably seen that it forces you to see it remarkably just as Cezanne makes you see a bowl of apples or Andrew Wyeth a muslin curtain blowing in at an open window. It is a face unlike any other face in all the world. All the faces in the world are in this one old face.[79]

The power of great art, whether the psalms, the parables, painting, or poetry, resides in its capacity to engage the whole person through encounter. That is why its insights continue to live in the hearts of the human family as defining sources of meaning. Our community has learned that philosophical discourse is no longer adequate to the task, that theological education is truncated without the art-making enterprise integrated. The vision of Koinonia is realized. Who after all are more uncommon bedfellows than the arts and the academy?

Where else besides works of art and constructs of religion do we find clues regarding matters of ultimacy? Whether delighted by nuanced insight concerning what we know or startled into recognition of what is not yet known, such moments of jarring intensity alive with transcendent luminosity are handed over to us by the religious and artistic communities. Face-to-face we confront symbolic representations of the nature of things: love and hate, alienation and wholeness, being and nothingness, the demonic and the divine, order and chaos, birth and death, the profound and the silly. Sadly, large segments of the religious community have refused hospitality to art's way of capturing and portraying essential essences of existence.

Because art as product and process is such a powerful ally, there is no substantive reason why a seminary or a church would not invite an artist-in-residence to the premise.[80] All it takes is a

---

79. Frederick Buechner, *Whistling in the Dark: An ABC Theologized* (San Francisco: Harper & Row, 1988).
80. See Linda Marie Delloff "Cathy Kapikian: A Seminary's Artist in Residence," *The Christian Century*, March 18–25, 1987, pp. 267–271.

commitment. Many competent, capable, and articulate artists are prime for this purpose. Of course monetary means vary, but lack of budget is no excuse. Time required on site as well as in-kind contributions are negotiable items. Assign a space, even if it is tiny, and thereby begin. Add hospitality and respect. Welcome a seminary artist-in-residence to audit classes and attend all campus functions. Whether hosted by a seminary or a church, an artist-in-residence will offer imaginative contributions in worship, education, fellowship, and outreach.

Think what would happen if a classroom in a church or any space in a seminary, the former often empty throughout the week yet in a heated building because of a working resident staff, became an artist's studio? Imagine the children on a Sunday or students during the week seeing the glorious mess of creation unfold. What would happen if adults were challenged and/or nurtured persistently by visual stimuli that companioned the Word? What if the religious community began to think seriously about the various aspects of the creative process and to treasure it as a reflection of being in the divine image?

Would a culture of creativity motivate a community to risk courageous action more confidently? Would a culture of creativity stimulate the naturally curious inclinations of our children? Would a culture of creativity give wings to the imagination, enabling leaps of faith?

What if people began to look upon the artist, as did twentieth-century British artist and teacher Eric Gill, not as a special kind of person, but instead began to look upon every person as a special kind of artist? What would happen if church leadership challenged those artists especially intent on freedom of expression, every kind of expression, to work alongside the curator/dealer/collector triad and create works for a caring community that knows that in the materiality of art, we find flickering glimpses of the Holy?

An advocacy role by the church for artistic expression in process and product is a wise commitment. In fact, the local parish provides an optimal setting for a resident artist and gives the congregation and artist alike the mutual benefit of each other's imaginings. Artists for consideration can be found in one's own neighborhood, district, county, region, etc. Alert your local arts council that you are seeking artists-in-residence and that your community will value their contributions. Hold a town meeting for the artists, listen, and exchange pertinent information.

One of the concerns of a church pursuing an artistic work and/or an artistic experience regards the issue of quality and standards. Well into my teaching career, a student surprised me with behavior that challenged a core value regarding this issue. I took a group to the National Gallery of Art. As we walked from one exhibition area to another, this student stopped abruptly, lingered over a work, and wept. She could not stifle her tears. Arresting her attention was a medieval four-foot devotional statue of the Virgin Mary. The work overwhelmed her.

Without thinking, my immediate response was one of annoyance. "Oh, goodness," I thought, "there's better work than this." Although it had made its way into the canon, my memory of Michaelangelo's *Pieta*, which I had encountered for the first time thirty-five years earlier in St. Peter's Basilica, flashed before my mind. My response at the time was identical to my student's. Emotion had welled uncontrollably. Nevertheless, I was dismissive of her response on the basis that this work capturing her attention was less than the best, teetering on sentimentality. "Get hold of yourself," I thought. Later that day driving home, and many times since, I have relived this experience.

Recently I had a similar experience. I spent Saturday afternoon watching and listening to *Samson and Delilah* at the Metropolitan Opera. In the last moment of the closing act, in a crescendo of music and movement, the pillar came toppling down. Embarrassingly, I lost control. My response was startlingly genuine and unexpected, as had been my student's.

We are derailed to the core by aesthetic experiences. Often such experiences arrive unexpectedly. One of the previous times for me occurred in the presence of the 5th century BCE bronze statue of the *Charioteer,* which I encountered in Athens. Another occurred in the Hague, as I stood in the presence of a very small painting of an old man bent over a table with his head in his hands. It was painted by Rembrandt.

I have never questioned my reactions, nor have I been dismissive of them. These kinds of encounters honor and define our humanness. The works that triggered my responses stand as master works. However, plagued by the memory of the genuine necessity of my student's response, my thinking has been turned topsy-turvy. Why should I, or she, or anyone for that matter, be beholden to the hierarchy of less, better, and best?

I am not endorsing mediocrity, nor am I abdicating standards. In fact, many of us hard-working artists are so shackled to the dictates imposed by elitist experts that we forever work under the plight of thinking our work is insufficient. The affliction runs deep. What would it be like to work without it? Perhaps others besides the artist and art connoisseurs should be concerned about standards. One such other might be an informed and supporting religious community that is willing to experience, experiment, and grow with an artist creating from within. Together, both artist and community would hold each other accountable, with the expectation that probing questions regarding standards of excellence are the responsibility of both.

Perhaps the whole art enterprise worldwide is analogous to the world's water sources. The size of an artist's influence is commensurate with the size of a body of water. Every millennium produces a few oceans of influence, a Michaelangelo, a Mozart. The influence of another bevy of artists impacts like a bay, a great lake, or a wide rolling river. But the world is also sustained by little rivers and their tributaries. The creeks, streams, and ponds count too, for they give life to those who encounter them. For the person who forever lives by the creek, that creek is as sustaining as is the ocean for the person who lives by it. So let us never forget the sustaining value of the creek.

The disruptions triggered by a storming ocean, a heaving bay, a swollen river, and a muddied creek are a metaphor for the artist's failed efforts, flawed attempts, fluke miscalculations, and banal blunders. Regardless of the magnitude of the artist's influence, whether it be from ocean to ocean or creek bed to its edge, all work is subject to flaws as well as perfections. While the ratio between the number of perfected works in relationship to failed works (mediated by the volume of work produced) defines greatness, the force of the ocean need not drown out the gurgling brook.

This musing reminds me of a pronouncement written by the eminent mid–twentieth-century art historian Ernst Gombrich. "There really is no such thing as Art. There are only artists."[81]

The sense of awe and wonder triggered by watching a resident artist work kindles the religious imagination. The reality of radical faith is brought to light when watching an artist trust a creative process to reveal resolution. The presence of grace is experienced as one watches an artist transform material and transcend the medium by creating a whole that is greater than the sum of its parts. The intermingling of creative processes with religious ideas is productive for the church and empowering for the artist. Build on the intrinsic relationship between the artistic and spiritual dimensions of human existence.

Although the following discussion sets forth parameters for a visual artist's residency in a church, its concepts are adaptable to residences of artists working in non-visual mediums (kinetic, poetic, dramatic, literary, and musical). Further, the issues and suggestions outlined in this discussion are pertinent to churches of differing membership size. Only slight modifications are required in establishing an artist-in-residence in a small church of approximately 200 members as opposed to a large church of 2,000 members.

Begin by establishing an arts committee. Congregations do not lack members interested in the arts. In a large church, it is politically astute to align the arts committee with another committee (worship, liturgy, education, or music) for support and status. As a catalyst for arts activity, the arts committee acts as communicator between professional staff, members of the congregation, and any persons engaged on behalf of the arts. This committee fans an organic welling-up of interest and activity from within the community.

Since the arts committee functions to enhance the life of the congregation through art otherwise dismissed or misunderstood, this committee must companion all of its programming

---

81. E. H. Gombich, *The Story of Art I* (New York: Phaidon, 1950), p. 5.

thoughtfully organic to its community. It must press a persistent educational agenda as already stated. First, however, the committee must educate itself well. Recognize that the multiple languages of worship (kinetic, poetic, dramatic, visual, literary, and musical) are imbedded in histories as well as contemporary utterances. Read and study for a while before fashioning programs. Then when programmatic initiatives commence, and, for instance, an artist arrives, the committee reminds the artist of the communal impulse undergirding much art of the past. It reminds the artist that the biblical view of what it means to be human is to engage in responsible action.

An organized study of several books bridging art and theology, art and religion, and art and spirituality enables church members to consider the validity or fallacy of categories connoted in such questions as: "What is religious art?"; "What is Christian art?"; "What is sacred art?"; and "What is liturgical art?"[82] These categories sign confusion between form and subject, style and content, and the how and the what of a work of art. Members will be prepared to point out invalid distinctions as well as to amplify meaningful ones. If asked, "Is the best church art the best secular art?" or "What purpose in Christianity should art serve?" or, "Can a non-Christian artist produce a work of art for liturgy?" committee members will answer by asking more questions. Compelled to such discourse with the congregation, committee members animate interest and understanding of the arts. They lay the groundwork for the appointment and arrival of an artist-in-residence.

It is wise to select an artist who is not only professionally competent but also articulate and engaging. Give the artist a space. Think out of the box, literally, with regard to the place. Artists transform closets. Convert a Sunday school classroom into a studio. Forty hours of working time on behalf of the church per month is an equitable exchange for a modest salary and in-kind contribution of space and utilities. Give the artist a key, and

---

82. Contact the Henry Luce III Center for the Arts and Religion at Wesley Theological Seminary for a current bibliography reflective of the issues pertinent to a church arts committee.

expect the artist to come and go at will, creating in the studio a place where the creative process is given high visibility. The congregation and the artist need at least a year together. A renewal contract or a contract with another artist is a viable option at the end of the first year.

Traditionalism versus innovation is the critical issue the church faces in committing to an artist-in-residence, and the arts committee will help the congregation understand this issue. The artist works at the boundary between tradition, that which is known and sustaining, and innovation, that which induces change. The latter introduces something new, which sometimes disrupts. By nature, a work of art has the capacity to take a person to a new place because the newness of the experience excites, distresses, delights, disturbs, or challenges.

In the last year of my Master's degree program at WTS, one month before graduation, I attended a weekly chapel service. To my horror, two students dressed as clowns were galloping up and down the center aisle on hobbyhorses. As worship unfolded, their antic gestures issued forth in bold swipes of lipstick on random congregants. This form of "artistic ministry" infuriated me. I rose abruptly and left. My deeply held Episcopalian conviction about the dignity of worship was disrupted. "Have I spent the last four years of my life for this?" All I could do was make a clown, and a larger than life one at that.

The following year when returning to the seminary as invited artist-in-residence to the faculty, I brought the clown with me and hung him on the studio wall opposing its double-door entrance. Shortly thereafter, I noticed a uniformed Army chaplain who would show up and linger at the entrance every Wednesday morning. One day he finally entered. "I have a clown ministry at the Walter Reed Army Medical Center on the Pediatric Oncology Ward. I wonder if we might borrow that clown."

Months later at the installation service on his ward, an eleven-year-old leukemia victim tethered to a portable IV clung to me. In a loud voice she announced emphatically to the gathered dignitaries, "I'm going to name him Charlie!"

Charlie became the medium for ministry. Traumatized children who could not speak spoke through Charlie while he endured the indignity of pretend needle punctures, chemotherapy, anesthesia, and surgery. Charlie, in his new setting, also ministered to me. For decades I have struggled with feelings of fear and helplessness brought on by my memories of stories and encounters in radiology departments with my medical doctor father, a cancer specialist. While it might have been smarter after that April chapel service to study the analytical concepts undergirding clown ministry, I sought instead an artistic response admittedly cathartic in process.

It took me years to discern the fact that the clowns are an art form in and of themselves, although one I do not like in the context I had experienced them. Initially, they wreaked havoc, propelling me in my own way to respond in a medium I knew. Who would have thought the new clown would give the children a companion, me liberation, and our seminary pride in a publicized extension ministry. The clowns, all three, ultimately evoked transformation.

The role of the artist, like that of the priest, is prophetic. Spiritual communities exist in the tension of what is and what is becoming. The artist and the priest are agents who mediate the Holy Spirit's disruptions as well as its peace making.

Whether disruptive or peaceful, the arts committee acts as mediator. It helps integrate the artist into the professional staff and advocates for the artist's inclusion in planning sessions. This achieves two things: first, the artist has time to incubate, a critical step in the creative process during which the artist wrestles with ideas and searches for solutions; second, the artist is not ghettoized. His or her work is seen as essential to the life of the church rather than "extra." If the artist is well integrated into the staff and understood and accepted as one of them, his or her visual proclamations will be taken in stride the same way the pastor's work is, whether the vision be comforting or disturbing. Remember, the sudden appearance of something unexpected in communal space can be lethal. Contrary to popular myth, an informed and therefore invested congregation rejoices in the creation of art, space enhancing or not, and even welcomes downright confrontational work.

Much variability exists, shaped for the most part by the work of the artist present. In the context of contemporary artistic practice, artists either maintain, negotiate, or destroy boundaries with their use of traditional mediums such as paint and clay and/or their use of modern materials such as plastic and laser light. Welcome all. Honor the artists who set out on explorations of unknown destination. At home in the world, they tinker with childlike wonder, ferret out what they discover, and embody it for us. Thus our world is ushered in through new ways of perceiving it, often ahead of their time. As a consequence, we never see the same way again.

Spiraling through the Guggenheim Museum in New York City forever changed the way I see, if not think about, trees. Mondrian's retrospective was my destination. Against a wall contiguous to a sloping ramp were approximately twenty paintings of Mondrian's trees hanging in historical sequence. The first was realistic and the last non-objective, a canvas of squares, rectangles, and lines. The intervening ones tracked the artist's unrelenting focus. No wonder my perception of trees was forever altered! Sojourns in Japanese Kabuki theatre accomplish the same thing for me. The smells of sushi lunch boxes, the extravagantly exaggerated costuming, and the repetitive thumping of clacking sound wedded simultaneously to the unfamiliar language of the voiced script, send me back to the streets better able to see and hear. This Westerner counts on kabuki every time she goes to Japan. Because art awakens our awareness in ways unique unto itself, the issue no longer is whether or not we welcome the artist. Rather, the issue is how tolerant we are to a diversity of artists among us.

The challenge for churches is to consider artists-in-residence who might work outside the bounds of perceived acceptable imagery within church contexts. If an artist is accustomed to designing temporary installations in user-friendly materials for fabrication by the community, then it is not too difficult to consider this artist as an artist-in-residence. As a condition of residency, expect him or her to create a temporary work for each liturgical season. The artist might devise a committee of approximately half a dozen members from the congregation to help envision what could happen in the sanctuary space around themes of worship. Referring to the appointed scripture, the artist might ask, "What does this scripture mean to you? What are the feelings this scripture evokes from you? What is the mood we are trying to get across with this theme?" These questions provoke a "feeling" response, enabling the artist to incubate ideas and solutions yielding works that speak center to center.

Another appointed group, with the aid of an annually budgeted materials allowance, might help paint, fabricate, cut, install, and otherwise construct the work designed by this resident artist. Thus the work in the sanctuary sometimes becomes the work of the people. This work, inspired by a theme emanating from a scriptural passage, might companion the processional, amplify the reading of the lessons, embellish a prayer, accompany the offering of the Communion elements, elaborate upon the sermon, or surface during the dismissal. The artist's job is to design the work, organize the project, work out mechanics of installation, and either construct it or instruct the people how to make it.

The artist embodies and incarnates the Word with the aid of the community in other ways too. He or she might offer intergenerational workshops during off-school times that are "how-to" in nature and thrive on the spontaneity of four-year-olds and seventy-year-olds working together. Other responsibilities might be retreats that lift up the creative process as a meditative process, sessions with Sunday school teachers, a chat or dialogue sermon on a Sunday morning about applied creativity as rootedness in the divine image. Contingent upon the artist's creative process and the consequences of it, challenge the artist unaccustomed to working liturgically to think liturgically on occasion, while simultaneously encouraging the artist accustomed to working liturgically to challenge the church with a wide range of art's issues. The resident artist keeps the community cognizant of the contemporary art scene. Expect the artist to share knowledge of art history, theory, and criticism. Think expansively. Reconsider traditional notions of what is appropriately placed in the narthex, sanctuary, and fellowship spaces. As a condition of the residency, have the artist leave a work when his or her time with your church ends. This is another way of keeping meaning-making alive.

The less obvious consequences of a relationship are more compelling. Gradually, the community senses the creative correspondences between things. For instance, the pastor is understood as standing before Scripture in the same way in which Van Gogh stood before the sunflower fields, Da Vinci before the Mona Lisa, or Rothko before a powerful sense of religious ecstasy. The pastor stands before the text confident that it has more to offer—more light to hurl into our darkness, more judgment to place on our infidelities, more grace to shed on what remains misshapen about us. Driven to proclaim this, he or she works much like the artist who images with paint the paradox of darkness within light animated by seeing a play of light across an empty room. The artist says, "I can't not do it," and the preacher adds, "The necessity has been laid upon me."

The resident artist connects the church to the local arts community. When networking commences, thoughts turn to gallery space in the church. In actuality, who would have thought a dozen years ago that churches would be allocating space for exhibiting art? This is a budding phenomenon. This idea's most ringing endorsement finds expression in the new Cathedral of Our Lady of the Angels, located in Los Angeles. The cavernous wall space of its ambulatory awaits the arrival of monumental works still to be commissioned, and some of its chapels remain totally unadorned, providing space for changing exhibitions of art.[83]

Much of the space inside many churches is a candidate for gallery space: narthex, foyers, hallways, fellowship halls, special meeting rooms, indeed the sanctuary itself. When a church undertakes this effort, the results are proportionate to the commitment. They can be exponential. A gallery focuses on the product of art-making. An artist-in-residence's commitment brings attention to the artist's process. Why not both for the benefit of all?

---

83. Ambulatory: an aisle surrounding the chancel of a church.

We will never know what will happen when we invite an artist-in-residence among us. Why not risk such relationships? Without risk, art and theology will not take us to an enlarged vision of reality where the imagination takes flight. People see faith embodied when they watch an artist trust a complex creative process to reveal resolution. Hope for things unseen is given a visible face. Do not truncate possibility by averting risk.

We are all in this adventure of living, together.

CHAPTER NINE

Integrating Art and Theology

*I*ntegrating art and theology occupies much of my adult life. Sometimes it is awkward. In a late afternoon appointment with my former academic dean, the sun filtered through the half-open blinds, slanting rigid parallel lines across his elongated tabletop. He sat at one end, I at the other. Surrounding us on three sides were walls embedded with shelves of floor to ceiling books, in their own way rigid and unyielding, their spines echoing the reflected parallel lines of light. The tension mounted. In a moment of exasperation, I yelped, "I am an artist first." Leaning into the table as his hand hit it, he retorted, "But you are a theologian too." Caught off guard, I peered at him in disbelief. "Really?" I said. "Yes, really."[84]

This self-induced skirmish realigned my thinking. When circumstances necessitate giving equal credence to both disciplines, equivocation is no longer necessary. Rather, a seamless integration is attempted. Such a situation arises when a work is relinquished to its context. On the one hand, the pastor, priest, or committee members, sometimes hesitantly, ask for a written statement of explication. On the other hand, most of today's artists would balk at the thought. If what the artist is commissioned to say is encoded successfully in an aesthetic form, then why the necessity for words? In fact, the whole point of capturing the essence of an idea through the materiality of a non-verbal medium is because it cannot be said the same by any other means. When working in community, however, the intention-

---

84. Dr. Douglas Meeks was Academic Dean at Wesley Theological Seminary from 1990 to 1998.

ality of the artist becomes an especially important ingredient of communication. Why not unmask the artist's process underlying his or her work?

When the reflecting that informs an artist's work is disclosed, it contributes to the dialogue not only between congregation and artist but also between one congregational member and another. Is this form of communication so radically different from that communicated in galleries and museums where titles lying alongside works hint at, if not open, a way into understanding them? And what of the reams of analytical materials written about a particular work of art? Must a line be drawn?

> If the meaning of a work of art cannot be expressed in words, I think one is entitled to wonder if it has *any* meaning. With sufficient effort and intelligence, I believe all meanings can be spoken. If the great religious mystics were able to communicate their insights verbally, it becomes idolatrous to regard the content of an admired object of art as incommunicable in words.[85]

Thoughtfully articulated words enable movement from one place to another. The necessity of this essential principle in facilitating the integration of art with theology in the seminary is imperative. I work alongside seminary scholars, sculpting discourse from an artistic point of view. Kneaded, pressed, and pushed, intransient mindsets of the past were displaced, including my own. Points of view between extremes folded in as well as participated in fresh conceptual configurations. Eventually a new creation emerged. Like a sculpture, this integration reflects surfaces with a seamless smoothing over of thumbprints squishing beneath it pockets of trapped air.

Leadership at the Henry Luce Foundation, keen observers and quintessential supporters of significant efforts in the field of art and theology, watched. Between 1990 and 1997, the Foundation

---

85. "Meaning in the Visual Arts," by artist Cleve Gray, *Yale Divinity School Reflections*, November 1981, Vol. 79, No. 1.

awarded our ever-expanding modes of integration with three sizable grants.[86] In 2000, the Foundation awarded us with a 1.7 million dollar endowment when the core curriculum faculty engaged artistic interpretation in the classroom and required artistic expression from the students as a response to learning.[87] At this time, our Center for the Arts and Religion, begun in 1983, was renamed after Henry Luce III.

In 2001, a nationally subscribed symposium titled "Trust the Arts to Speak" was convened. The Henry Luce III Center for the Arts and Religion (LCAR) invited sixteen designated fellows, each of whom had long histories in the field of art and theology, to participate.[88] Martin Marty was the keynote speaker. At its close, the invited fellows convened in a two-and-a-half hour panel discussion which Wilson Yates, then president of the United Theological Seminary of the Twin Cities and editor of *Arts: The Arts in Religious and Theological Studies*, moderated. The panel responded to the following question: what is the one challenge that you see facing art and theology in the future?[89] Following are some of the responses.

Yates began by saying, "One of the figures who is parent of the whole effort is Bob Seaver, a scholar who taught at Union.... He could not be here although he is a fellow, but participants from Union have brought him through another medium." In an eight-minute videotape interview that took place in 1997, Bob Seaver spoke of his work in drama and then said:

---

86. In 1995, the seminary's faculty committee on theology and the arts prepared and circulated a document defining guidelines by which the faculty could evaluate artistic work created by students and guidelines by which students could approach and accomplish an artistic response to an assignment.

87. For a detailed description of integration in a seminary classroom see "The Arts, Midrash, and Biblical Teaching," in *Arts, Theology, and the Church: New Intersections*, edited by Kimberly Vrudny and Wilson Yates (Pilgrim Press, 2005), pp. 105–124. For a detailed description of seminary integration, see "Wesley Theological Seminary and the Arts," in *Arts: The Arts in Religious and Theological Studies*: Seven Two, 1995, pp. 4–8.

88. For a detailed description of this event, see *ARTS: The Arts in Religious and Theological Studies*, Fifteen One, 2003, pp. 46–47.

89. A transcript and video of the Fellows Panel Discussion is available through The Henry Luce III Center for the Arts and Religion at WTS.

Amos Wilder came up with a wonderful statement about the church, the arts, and contemporary culture.... He stated four very important tasks of the church...to know contemporary culture and its expressions and through them know our time more fully...accept and interpret them in terms of Christian criteria...contribute directly to the health and vitality of the arts and the proper understanding of the vocation of the artist...and heal the breach that has arisen between the religious institution and those chiefly identified with the arts in our society.... In our day these same tasks are before the church and before theological education.

Frank Burch Brown built upon the task of healing the breach between the arts and the church by reminding everyone that learning needs to take place on both sides. Paul Westermeyer contextualized the idea by stating that seminaries need to deal with history, praxis, and formation simultaneously, while noting, "It's not 'trust the arts to speak,' but 'what will the arts say!'" Darius Swann concluded, "As purveyors of theological

education, we are probably going to have to change, modify, and enlarge our concept of how we learn, and I'm speaking now of the Western predilection and especially the Protestant predilection for ear over eye...not taking the analytical as normative." John Dillenberger questioned,

> Have we paid enough attention to the way in which the arts are distinct, give something different? Where is theology today? There is no single ideology, there are only theologies, and they differ and move around in different ways.... In California, there is no religious or ethnic majority. That is a sign of the future. How are we going to deal with this diversity? Dare we hope that maybe the arts can be one of the ways in which there can be rapprochement among these cultures?... This will change theology as we have known it.... This will change the nature of churches as we know them today.

Janet Walton perceived herself "as a coach who puts into place things which can happen...use the context in which we find ourselves as a teaching partner.... I have been very mindful since 9/11 of what people have done in the city, and not just with words, through the lens of the artists…our responsibility is to bring the theological community into conversation with them." Judith Rock spoke,

> One gift and challenge the arts bring to the academy is the intent and insistent, relentlessly messy physicality in which the arts live and by which the artists make, whether we're talking about dancer, writer, organist, or sculptor.… I think this is the essential issue when there is a conflict between the academy and the arts. We want an equal partnership without the hierarchy of this way of knowing as valid, better, more fruitful than that way of knowing.

Diane Apostolos-Cappadona said, "the greatest danger in seeing people who do interdisciplinary studies—religion and art, art and theology—is that the arts are not taken in and of themselves, they are taken as illustration. Take them as exempla."

While relatively small, the cadre of scholars working in theology and art maintains a lively discussion through their publications, and now a significant number of books proliferate. If the conversations inherent to them exist for their own sake, may they continue to discourse on integration and reflect on initiatives. If the conversations exist for the sake of the church, they must argue for administrative leadership in theological schools to formulate positions in the arts. And some of these positions must be open to artists, just as the conversation must invite their presence. Lodging an argument to the contrary, based on the rhetoric that a non-scholarly presence or a practically-oriented, rather than theoretically-oriented, initiative is inimical to a school's tradition, is flawed. Dr. G. Douglass Lewis, President of WTS from 1982 to 2002, wholeheartedly supported and fueled this artist's presence and initiatives. The experiences related in this book are the consequences.

Poised to participate in such conversations is the leadership (college and university studio art professors, art historians,

and outstanding freelance artists) of CIVA, Christians in the
Visual Arts. Celebrating in 2005 its 25th year of existence,
CIVA's leadership has instigated a revolution in our culture.
CIVA's leadership has earned their place at the theologian's
table.[90]

Begun out of a felt need for one another because the art world
dismissed, shunned, or ostracized the artist working from a
faith perspective, this organization prospered. Maintaining the
highest artistic standards, over time CIVA's biennial national
conferences, regional workshops, juried exhibitions, traveling
exhibitions, stunning and articulate publications, and illustrated directory garnered notice. Curators, dealers, collectors,
and critics now pay attention. So might the church. CIVA is a
deep well of talent, ideas, and possibility. Prime the pump and
draw the water.[91]

A relatively new participant in integrating art and theology is
MOBIA, the Museum of Biblical Art, at Broadway and 61st St.,
New York, NY. Touted as New York City's newest museum, it
inhabits a larger, redesigned space at the former site of the
Gallery at the American Bible Society. That society's rare scripture collection is now on long-term loan to this museum. One
of MOBIA's four changing exhibitions for 2005 included an
exhibition titled "The Next Generation: Contemporary
Expressions of Faith." About this show, MOBIA's print material stated:

> The contemporary art world often overlooks
> works of art inspired by the Bible. Yet artists
> continue to explore religious themes and sym-
> bolism despite reduced patronage in an
> increasingly secularized society.... The work

---

90. CIVA, by its own admission in its print material, is "the premier visual
arts organization connecting the artist, the church, and the culture." The
work of CIVA artists can be seen and its history read in *Faith and Vision:
Twenty Five Years of Christians in the Visual Arts*, published by Square
Halo Books, Inc., 2005, Baltimore, MD.

91. For a competent discussion of the museum world's changing attitude
towards exhibiting religious art, see "Religion on a Pedestal: Exhibiting
Sacred Art" by Ena Giurescu Heller, in *Reluctant Partners: Art and Religion in Dialogue*, edited by Ena Giurescu Heller (New York: The Gallery
of the American Bible Society, 2004), pp. 122–138.

of 44 artists (CIVA members) on display illustrates the continuing relevance of religion to
artistic production as well as the vital role art
plays in the testament of faith.[92]

Another aspect of integrating art and theology regards the current education of art historians. Now, the theological and spiritual influences underpinning an artist's body of work are
considered in art history curriculums. This is a relatively new
phenomenon.

Such a focus undergirds a course I teach entitled "Van Gogh
and God: The Artist as Spiritual Guide." *The Letters of Vincent
Van Gogh*, selected and edited by Ronald de Leeuw, is required
reading, and in it, students discover a wounded healer. In his
paintings, students discover images that express a profound
spirituality often absent in works with explicitly religious subject matter. Exploding with the immanence of divinity, Van
Gogh's paintings reflect his lifelong search for his ground of
being. Through the process of painting, he acted out his lifelong quest.[93] Students see the difference between traditional
painting embodying a shared orthodoxy, painting illustrating
the sacred story, and painting which scintillates with a sense of
the sacred but eschews encoding in religious doctrine, dogma,
or story. Students meet an artist who applies paint driven by a
sacramental sensibility. They mourn over his failures, yet marvel at his quest for discernment. In Letter 531, they read,

> So, I am always caught between two currents
> of thought, firstly, material difficulties, turn-
> ing this way and that to make a living, and
> then, the study of colour. I keep hoping that
> I'll come up with something. To express the
> love of two lovers by the marriage of two com-
> plementary colours, their blending and their
> contrast, the mysterious vibrations of related

---

92. Found in MOBIA's *Schedule of Exhibitions* brochure for 2005.
93. Cliff Edwards, Van Gogh and God: A Creative Spiritual Quest (Chicago:
Loyola University Press, 1989). Edwards succeeds in the unprecedented
task of thoroughly analyzing the theological and spiritual significance of
Van Gogh's works.

tones. To express the thought of a brow by the
radiance of a light tone against a dark background. To express hope by some star. Someone's passion by the radiance of the setting
sun. That's certainly no realistic trompe l'oeil,
but something that really exists, isn't it?[94]

Sometimes discussions of integration lead to unexpected outcomes. Following is an example of what happens when an
artist and a theologian accept the perils of collaboration. After
more than a decade of team teaching with church historian
Dr. Arthur D. Thomas, Jr., fresh insights gleaned from one
another still outweigh the occasional glitch. The tug and pull
of shared discussions in our course titled "Art and Spirituality: The Image in Historical Context" invigorate course content. We examine the challenge of images to Christian
devotion from the catacombs to the present, and look at the
influence of particular schools of spirituality on art and
artists. We view art as an important dimension for spiritual
formation, and beauty as a foundation for the moral life. For
example, a shared session in the classroom studies the spirituality of Teresa of Avila as reflected in projected images of
Bernini's sculpture. In all sessions, we maintain a running
commentary on how to see.

Following one lively three-hour session, I remarked that we
should see Italian sites together. Meaning just the two of us, I
was startled when Dr. Thomas returned the following week
with a scenario including students. The following year, we went
to Italy, taking in tow students who earned degree credits as a
consequence. We stood in holy places where a school of spirituality no longer existed as a theoretical abstraction. We saw it
embodied, as in the Arena/Scrovegni Chapel frescos in Padua
and also in Fra Angelico's cycle of frescos at the St. Marco
Dominican monastery in Florence. There St. Dominic's (the
founder of Dominican spirituality) positions of prayer were
frescoed on the cells' walls. We stood in holy places where art,

---

94. Ronald de Leeuw, ed., The Letters of Vincent Van Gogh, trans. A.
Pomerans (London: Penguin, 1996), p. 395. Trompe l'oeil is a style of
painting in which objects are depicted with photographically realistic
detail.

instead of being a projected shadow of itself, was real and inspired by spiritual context, as in Da Vinci's *Last Supper*. Da Vinci painted this masterwork as if the source of light diffused across the apostles enters through the refectory windows where it resides. There, monks shared meals in the painted presence of Christ partaking of his last supper.

Since our first trip to Italy, we have taken students to France, Switzerland, and Germany, and another time to Ireland, Wales, England, and Scotland. Bracketing the former trip were Grüenwald's Isenheim altar piece in Colmar and Lucas Cranach the Elder's painted altar pieces in the Church of St. Maren in Wittenberg. In Colmar, students saw an agonizing portrayal of the Crucifixion in which Jesus' body is racked by a deadly disease of the sixteenth century. It is seen in the context of the monk's hospital where it, along with its visual counterparts inclusive of a joyous scene of the Resurrection, ministered to the patients afflicted with the same disease. Theologian Karl Barth kept a reproduction of this work in his study and wrote on its theological import.[95] In Wittenberg we saw visual evidence (Luther himself is pictured in a pulpit preaching before a crucified Christ and is pictured in the *Last Supper* as one of the apostles) of Luther's appreciation for art in worship space, unlike Calvin's Geneva where we saw his visually stark auditory embodying the Reformed fear of idolatry.

Bracketing the later trip were Dublin's *Book of Kells* and the Island of Iona, known as a thin place.[96] In Dublin, seeing this illuminated Gospel and later the Lindisfarne illuminated Gospel illustrated Celtic Christianity's rare flowering of visual creativity in a time when much of the rest of Europe was in the Dark Ages. In the mystical physical environment of Iona with its Celtic ruins, students visited local artists carrying on the visual tradition of Celtic Christianity. Today's recovery of this tradition reintroduces a love, respect, and reverence for the natural world. Celtic prayers mediate an enchanting divine/human rapport around especially ordinary moments of living.

---

95. Karl Barth, introduction and epilogue by John D. Godsey, *How I Changed My Mind* (Edinburgh: The Saint Andrews Press, 1969) pp. 11, 26.
96. Thin places are places where the human family discerns the veil between ourselves and the Holy as very transparent.

These on-site visits showing images in historical context, some rarely included in standard pilgrimage tours, persuaded fellow travelers (The Ecumenical Institute of Theology of St. Mary's Seminary in Baltimore co-sponsors these trips with Wesley Theological Seminary) that the human imagination is boundlessly inventive in its ways of visually mediating lived experience of the Divine.

In 2005, we returned to Italy, and two WTS faculty colleagues joined as passengers. We invited one, Dr. Laurence H. Stookey, to give a lecture titled "The Church as the Heavenly Jerusalem: An Introduction to Architectural Meaning." Our wired tour bus accommodated our many lectures.

Dr. Stookey gave a riveting lecture pertinent to the pre-Reformation sites about to be visited. "To go to church is to go to heaven," said Dr. Stookey, "This was one facet of a set of common assumptions then which may seem foreign to some of us today." He discoursed on how New Testament writing and the early church adapted the platonic notion of ideal categories, and in particular how a church structure became the embodiment of a striving after an ideal form. "The things you are about to see," he said, "but may not *truly see* are a striving after the whole heavenly city of the new Jerusalem itself, coming down out of heaven from God."[97]

As our bus rolled along, he continued his engaging description of architectural detail, both inside and outside, to ensure that fellow travelers would comprehend (truly see) the intentionality behind what would be seen. He began with the church towers, emblematic of the skyline of the celestial city, and concluded with the interior dome, its dark-blue sky and gold stars emblematic of a renewed and shining creation. He regaled us with witty commentary on the architectural statuary that greets the worshiper, the Christ in Judgment in the tympanum who reminds those who enter that judgment is mediated before one enters the Holy City, and discoursed on the great cloud of levitating witnesses who adorn the interior fresco and mosaic walls. He bombarded our minds with extravagant visual detail and supported his thesis with scriptural evidence. What startled me was his conclusion. He said:

---

97. See Revelation 21:2.

In my seminary course "Introduction to Corporate Worship," I require all students to attend a service in one of the Eastern Orthodox bodies. They are to write a report of the visit, but I give them almost no clue as to what to expect in these churches where at least some form of Platonism still holds sway. In what may seem counter-intuitive, particularly for those students from Protestant traditions for whom highly decorated church buildings are quite alien, they tell me again and again: "It was so beautiful. Why, it felt just like being in heaven." Precisely! Is there any hope, or any need, for bringing back in some form the idea that to go to church is to go to heaven? Without any suggestion that Platonic philosophy needs to be reinstated, I think so. This seems particularly so in churches where the Eucharist is becoming more central and frequent, and where it is understood to be our earthly anticipation of eating and drinking together at the great feast of heaven at the end of time. Should liturgical action at the Lord's Table and artistic visualization in the building that houses the Holy Table be divorced? I hope not, but only time will tell.

CHAPTER TEN

Integrating Art and Theology in Context: DVD Images

The enclosed DVD contains images of my work created through the years. They are embodiments of theological thought integrated with artistic means.[98] The seven chapters organizing this work contain the following titles. (Please refer to the appendix for the subtitles to the chapters and the lists of churches, organizations, or institutions that commissioned the works shown in the DVD.)

1. Transforming Liturgical Space

2. Transforming Other Ecclesial Space

3. Paraments and Vestments

4. Temporary Installations

5. Banners

6. Creative Process

7. Designs of Works in Progress

---

98. My work has been exhibited in seventeen juried, nationally advertised call-for-entries exhibitions. Five were IFRAA (Interfaith Forum on Religion, Art, and Architecture) Biennial Exhibitions, in three of which I received a merit award. I have juried two other nationally advertised call-for-entries exhibitions, in one of which I was the sole juror. It was CIVA's 1997 "Celebrating the Sacred in Contemporary Textile Art," and it toured the USA for the following two years. I designed, fabricated, and installed in 1998 a public art installation of the ART IN PUBLIC PLACES PROGRAM OF THE CITY OF GAITHERSBURG. This textile work, comprised of fourteen double-sided, juxtaposed banners of different lengths, hangs in the entrance of the grand lobby of the Gaithersburg Activities Center at Bohrer Park. It is a place-making work, as it reflects back, through cutouts and abstract imagery in opaque blocks of color, on historical sights in the city.

Most of the work is designed and fabricated by myself, as for instance the first work pictured, and some of the work is the consequence of participatory aesthetics.

Chapters 1, 2, and portions of 3 and 4 show the context in which a work exists and sometimes show the context prior to the installation of a work. When multiple works exist in the same context, they are organized liturgically and commence with the season of Advent.

Chapter 2, "Transforming Other Ecclesial Space," is divided as follows: Narthex, Balcony, Sanctuary Entrance, Chapel, Church Hallway, and Fellowship Hall. In actuality, the work shown under the subdivision of church hallway took its impulse from children's images. This work resides in the entrance hallway of a church's daycare center.

Chapter 3, "Paraments and Vestments" is divided as follows: Paraments, Paraments and Vestments, and Vestments. Sometimes only paraments were commissioned, other times only vestments as in the chasuble that took its design impulse from St. Francis' "Canticle of Brother Sun Sister Moon" and the Episcopalian cope that took its design impulse from Ephesians 3:20. Sometimes paraments and vestments were commissioned together, to be in relationship.

Chapter 4, "Temporary Installations," is divided as follows: Convention Centers, Retreat Centers, and Outdoor Sites. The first work interprets seven hymn texts in seven separate 25' long divisions. The banner mobile celebrated the new United Methodist Hymnal in Constitution Hall. Surprisingly, it rotated continuously throughout the event due to the air currents generated by the multiple voices in song. The last work in this chapter is the three-sided altar frontal and its bracketing banners created for Walter Reed Army Medical Center's Easter morning sunrise service.

Chapter 5, "Banners," begins with groups of banners designed as a unit. The chapter ends with banners conceived as single entities. In their aggregate, they show a diversity of design approaches reflective of client expectations. Some are traditional, conservative because of the context or community, others abstract. Some bear images on both sides. Most are early works.

Chapter 6, "Creative Process," offers the viewer a glimpse into my studio and the creative processes undertaken within it. Twenty years ago, a faculty colleague challenged me to document my creative process. Since that time, I have documented several creative processes because students found the first documentation helpful. When they see a creative process undertaken from its inception to its completion, they discern the artist's way of materializing an impulse, idea, and/or train of thought.

Chapter 7, "Designs of Works in Progress," begins with in-scale paper designs for paraments that will reside in front of the needlepointed reredos, comprised of a rectangular center with bracketing roundels (Kennedy Heights Presbyterian Church), pictured in chapter 1. The last two works in the chapter are being needlepointed by the community. I will paint the 45" square wooden slatted interior of the latter 9' in diameter work. All entries in this chapter, with the exception of the face of Jesus, are works of participatory aesthetics; communities are fabricating them.

As noted in chapter 9 of this book, explication of an artwork invites a privileged dialogue, enhancing a shared experience between artist and viewer. Portions of what I wrote and presented to the commissioning communities regarding selected works in each chapter of the DVD follow. In no instance are statements included regarding how a particular work integrates with the architecture of a space. Having written a chapter detailing such matters in theory, the illustrations will provide evidence but none will tell the whole story.

The explanations provided in this chapter evolved from ongoing conversations held with myself while creating a work. Initially reflective in nature, they metamorphosed into didactic thought when pressed to write words of explanation. As such, they are a stretch from the work they describe. Consider them as you will, but finally lay them aside in favor of simply looking at the work.

DVD Chapter 1: Transforming Liturgical Space

The first work shown is 37' long and is comprised of painted, stained, and inlaid wood panels of several depths. Its size and shape echo the shape of the balcony front at a right angle to it and the horizontal band of stained glass windows opposing it. Spread across its wooden surface is the image of water. Each liturgical season is visually expressed when a set of appliquéd wool panels becomes visible by the removal of wood panels under which the appliquéd panels are hidden. Sometimes other appliquéd panels, kept in storage, also are slotted into the wood structure as the liturgical season changes. During Holy Week, and for some weddings, the reredos is seen without appliqué panel inserts. The surface image of water on the wooden foundation continues in continuity in all of the appliquéd wool panels through visual transparencies. This way of imaging is easily seen in the pictures of the separate sets of liturgical panels photographed outdoors. When placed in the wood structure, they separate one from another.

> The common substance of water is a reminder in creation of the work and love of our Creator. Through such signs as water, the material world can be a means of revelation. At the left of the center platform is a suggestion of the watery chaos of the beginning. This creation image is a sign that water, stirred by the Spirit, contains the life-giving, creative force of God present in Genesis 1. Over the center of the platform is a suggestion of the Flood, wherein the world was recreated after sin. This image of Deluge points to the idea that water both destroys and renews. Thus the water of baptism becomes a symbol of judgment as well as creation. At the right of the center platform is an image of the River Jordan suggesting Christ's baptism, that convergence of divine and human life wherein a second creation is realized. Christ is the new creation and through Him and our baptism we are newly created in

covenant community. The stream of water entering in the upper right suggests the life-giving force of the waters of our own baptism.

We who gather to worship in the presence of this work come as the baptized and partake of the shared memory, wisdom, and tradition imparted through the liturgical seasons of Advent, Christmas, Epiphany, Lent, Easter, Pentecost, and Ordinary Time.

The second work shown in Chapter One, a 25'x10' needle-pointed reredos, yields insights at several levels. Following a statement concerning the tripart symbol of God in its upper register, the symbols of the disciples in the descending registers, and the symbolic variations of the cross for each liturgical season in the lower registers, the conclusion stated:

From Advent through the time following Pentecost we are called to worship in the knowledge that the God in whom we place our trust has come to us in human form. At another level of perception the circle, an archetypal symbol of eternity, intermingles with other symbolically suggestive motifs such as the fleur-de-lis and diamond to create an intricate visual metaphor for the interdependence of creation.

The third work also is a needlepointed reredos comprised of a central rectangular piece with a circle form (roundel) bracketing each of its sides. The Trinity is symbolized in the three pieces by the six pointed star on the left, the cross in the center, and the descending dove on the right. The wooden cross appended to the center piece was bequeathed to the church in 1963, its incorporation a condition of the commission. All three pieces are comprised of a single repetitive square, 6" in size in the roundels and 7½" in size in the center rectangular piece. Every square, whether 6" or 7½", contains the same nine curvilinear shapes.

Variation is achieved by rotating, mirror imaging, and stacking these squares with the erasure of some of the lines dividing the shapes within each square. Their coloration followed no rules other than the dictates of my imagination. Not only did the use of a repetitive cell of design simplify greatly for the volunteers the transfer of the design onto canvas, but it also provided a compelling means for constructing a visual statement of Trinity. Its three parts, Creator, Redeemer, and Sustainer stand separately, yet are comprised of the same design substance.[99]

The fourth work, another reredos, is seen in its completed form only during Ordinary Time. The rest of the year it is seen in the process of becoming. In its completed state its component parts are submerged into a larger design aggregate echoing to some extent the abstract design characteristics of the stained glass windows. These windows bear no symbolism and reside above eye level while the reredos bears symbolism and resides at eye level. The reredos is always viewed from a distance, never up close.

Reluctant to work in this space, I initially refused. When I returned a year later, I discovered that the feeling provoked by the space (which I thought was stunning) was, according to the committee, "lacking." In the discussion that ensued, they shared their frustration that the color and light symbolic of God's presence reigned above them. They wanted God's presence mediated through particular symbols at eye level sight. Consequently, the following accompanied this work's installation:

> Our Creator gave us color and our world
> rejoices in it. Through color and symbol, this
> reredos proclaims the Word of God by imag-
> ing sacred events remembered through liturgy.

---

99. Susan Kitchen, a member of Kennedy Heights Presbyterian Church in Cincinnati, Ohio, was the indispensable project manager. After its installation in October 2004, she wrote an articulate piece detailing technical aspects of the project with a time line related to the achievement of each aspect. Her guidance was exceptional, from the inception of the project to its installation. In the spring of 2005, she wrote to me the following, "I found an experienced needlepoint appraiser through the Cincinnati Art Museum, and she came from Dayton to look at the work. I made a detailed list of money expenses and volunteer hours put into the project. She was much impressed with the pieces, and the outcome is that she has appraised them for $88,500, which our insurance company has accepted." Presently Susan is supervising as well as sewing the paraments I am designing to reside in front of the reredos.

In this unfolding visual drama, the Advent panels anticipate the inbreaking of the Kingdom of God. The presence of light and crown in one panel, and the presence of the Advent crosses in the other (minus their upper arm these crosses acknowledge Old Testament scripture yet to be fulfilled by New Testament writing) anticipate the fulfillment of prophetic writing. The angelic figure points to movement between the heavenly and earthly spheres.

Christmas is represented by "the ox knows its owner, and the ass its master's crib."[100] Placed under the Christmas Star, the letters IHS further point to the miracle of this Child. The other Christmas panel yields an image of the gate of Jerusalem and baptismal shell, the latter symbol associated with Epiphany and the manifestation of the divinity of Christ.

The story of Holy Week emerges through familiar Lenten imagery. The palms thrown by the multitudes that welcomed Christ but later rejected him coexist with symbols of the Last Supper, grapes and wheat. On the other panel, the cross of crucifixion is punctuated with thorns, tossed dice, and Judas's coins.

The Easter panel resides at the center and yields an image of Calvary while simultaneously pointing to resurrection. The former makes the latter possible.

The panel bearing the symbolic presence of Pentecost resides above the representation of Easter. Through color and movement, it portrays a sense of tongues of fire and gifts of the Spirit.

The last liturgical season, the time after Pentecost, is visualized in three panels containing the six-pointed star of creation, a Trinity

---

100. Isaiah 1:3.

symbol, and the Alpha and Omega. The latter
is derived from scripture. It suggests that God
as Creator, revealed to us through Christ and
present to us through the Holy Spirit, is with
us from beginning to end.

Although the reredos was designed and fabricated by myself,
the paraments beneath it were designed by myself and fabricated by the community. Their diverse shapes reflect their relationship to the reredos's volumes and voids, which change with
each liturgical season.

The fifth work is a 60' long set of needlepointed kneelers. At
the entrance of the sanctuary is a large baptismal font not far
from the kneelers. Overlaying the entire surface of the kneelers
is a sense of moving water in transparency. This complex work
bears images of the salvation story unfolding from one cushion
to the next. It commences at one corner with the watery chaos
of the beginning and ends at the fourth corner with a cushion
imaging the season after Pentecost. In the short section
between these two corners are cushions bearing the names of
the church and a cushion combining symbols for consecrations
and confirmations. The latter is interchangeable with a cushion
used for weddings. Initially, the church was given a linear, in-
scale drawing of the entire work mounted on a board approximately 5' on its vertical side. Under the drawing of each
cushion was an explanation.

The sixth work of multiple liturgical banners is a work of participatory aesthetics. There are no pictures on the DVD of the
banners' back sides, all sixty of which bear images. When worship was completed and congregants turned to leave, they saw
either a duplication of the image closest to the altar in the
series, or a new image on the back side of each banner.

The context for the eleventh work is the lowest floor of a senior health care facility located in a large retirement village. This
work resides in an all-purpose space. In its closed form, it provides a surface onto which notices and crafted works are tacked.
Underneath it, plastic bowling pins sometimes sit, challenging
nearby seniors in wheelchairs to toss a plastic ball. On Sunday
mornings, it swings open in less than a minute, and the nearby

furniture on casters, now uncovered, is pushed in front of it. Thus a utilitarian space becomes a worship space. The work when opened is bold, easy to see, and tactile. For the benefit of the residents, a written explication of the work appears weekly in bold typeface on the back page of the worship bulletin.

The thirteenth work resides in a synagogue. It is a huppah. The huppah, whether wedding tent, shared prayer shawl, or bridal canopy, occupies the ritual space of a Jewish marriage ceremony.

> This huppah celebrates holy matrimony through its visualization of the sacred text, Song of Solomon. In its literal interpretation passionate lovers intermingle with motifs derived from the flora, fauna, and cityscapes described in the poetry. In its symbolic interpretation visual vignettes tell of the relationship between God and Israel. Both interpretations exist in tradition. In the literal imagery of the lower tier, visual transparencies of entwined lovers mingling with motifs such as a bramble bush, a vineyard, or the walls of Jerusalem capture the scripture's rich layers of meaning. In the allegorical imagery of the upper tier, overlays of an eagle (symbolic of God in Hebrew Scripture) mingling with illustrations of Israel's history from Exodus to Exile extol God's love for the beloved, the people of Israel. In both tiers, the movement of shapes in subtle colors from one panel to another captures the lyrical and sensual quality of this love poem.
>
> In the literal visualization of the lower tier, two registers image love dialogues, poems expressing conversations between two lovers. The third register images love monologues, poems spoken to or about the beloved, and the fourth register images both. All of them communicate the pathos, longing, and unbridled passions characteristic of the poems.

In the original statement of explication, thirteen poems from the text were quoted. They were the source of inspiration for the panels of literal content. Following are two of the poems:

> The fig tree puts forth its figs,
>   and the vines are in blossom;
>   they give forth fragrance.
> Arise, my love, my fair one,
>   and come away.

and

> Make haste, my beloved,
>   and be like a gazelle
>   or a young stag
>   upon the mountain of spices.[101]

The panels filled with people in each register of the lower tier represent the Song's chorus who echo the refrain, "Eat, O friends, and drink: drink deeply, O lovers!"[102]

The symbolic images highlighting the history of the relationship between God and Israel from Exodus to Exile echo the theme found in two texts, one from Exodus and the other from Isaiah. Exodus 19:4 reads "...and how I bore you on eagles' wings and brought you to myself," and Isaiah 40:31 reads, "But they who wait for the LORD shall renew their strength, they shall mount up with wings like eagles." The latter expresses the people's initiative towards God and the former expresses God's initiative towards the Israelites. Thus the movement of God through human life is portrayed by the eagle overlaying illustrations unique to Israelite history.

---

101. Song of Solomon 2:13, 8:14.
102. Song of Solomon 5:1.

The following themes appear in the upper tier's four registers. The panels filled with people in each register symbolize the people of Israel.

Exodus: Miriam and her Tambourine

Sustenance in the Wilderness: Quails

Covenant on Mt. Sinai: Moses and the Decalogue

A Land Flowing with Milk and Honey: Olive Trees

Kingship and Nationhood: Star of David and Menorah

The Prophets: "But let justice roll down like waters, and righteousness like an ever-flowing stream"[103]

Exile: Figure in Lament

Hope in the Midst of Exile: Make a Joyful Noise

DVD Chapter 2: Transforming Other Ecclesial Space

The following accompanied the presentation of the design of the first work pictured:

> In the shadow of Calvary lurks our Resurrection God. From the darkness rises the promise of possibility. Couched in the swirling shifting hues, values, and intensities of color, this work yields the mystery that God is at once Creator, Redeemer, and Sustainer. It is a visible sign that the Holy, symbolically encountered in the narthex, is found concretely in this place through spiritual encounter.

In this work of participatory aesthetics, one volunteer was a Muslim woman whose family was aided by the parish as part of a refugee resettlement program. She participated as her way of expressing gratitude for support of herself and her family. After

---

103. Amos 5:24.

being reminded by a family member that the tapestry contained Christian symbols, she responded, "It's the same God."[104]

The second work, *God of the Waters*, was titled by the presiding pastor. It references the theme of baptism.

The sixth work comprised of four units of differently colored frames-interprets the 104th Psalm.

The tenth work-images the burning bush: "And the angel of the LORD appeared to him in a flame of fire out of the midst of a bush…"[105] The outside edges of the end panels of this three-panel work reside away from the wall. The center panel plus the inside edges of each bracketing panel fit flat against the wall. This framing mechanism engenders a sense of engulfment for those who stand in its presence.

When designing this work I wondered what Moses' sandals looked like. Not knowing, I glanced down at my own feet, kicked off the sandals I was wearing, and used them as a guide. Throughout the work, hundreds of French knots were sewn to create a sparkling effect. What an impossibly harsh task this was. Try sewing a French knot through 100% wool fabric bonded to a strong canvas. Never again!

The last work in this chapter is an interpretation of the last chapter in the Book of Revelation. It is 7' x 17½' x 5" and is divided into four units, each with two hinged panels. It takes the place of a curtain on the stage of a fellowship hall.

> The Book of Revelation was written initially to give comfort and courage to Christians in Asia Minor in time of trouble. How did the reading and study of it inform this work, and more importantly, how does the visual vocabulary utilized in this work enable us to experience sympathetically the eschatological vision?[106] Drawing on the last chapter for inspiration, I felt it

---

104. Told to me by Reverend John A. Shaffer, Grace Episcopal Church, Baldwinsville, NY.
105. Exodus 3:2.
106. Eschatology: doctrines concerning the end times.

incumbent upon myself to risk a courageous statement. John of Patmos challenges us to be as creative in our imagination as he is with his. I hope it invites your imaginative interaction.

We begin by encountering images couched in symbols, the meaning of which is implicit in the text, guessed at by their location in the book, or figured out by their relationship to first-century mythologies. John proclaimed metaphorically a remarkable transformation. He writes of power and conquest through images of suffering. The visual metaphor for this assertion is seen in the gentle lamb ensconced in the throne chair and cradled by the winged spirits of God. Through suffering and weakness, the victim becomes the victor. This primary revelation is threaded throughout the book. Both the original texts and this work rely on the use of worldly images. Stream, tree, chair, fruit, leaves, lamb, beast, etc., show the character of the eternal.

We also discover in this text a world filled with images sharply contrasting, dark and light, good and evil, Christ and the Antichrist. We experience satanic force vis-à-vis the Beast who "was given a mouth uttering haughty and blasphemous words,"[107] and we see this beast nipping at the angelic interceptor of God. In this eschatological vision of the eternal reign of God, evil is defeated, inverted, turned upside down.

The goodness of this world is amplified in the next. The perfect symmetry of the renewed Holy City is described by John as a cube. Heaven appears perfectly proportioned. The precious stones by which the city is built shine with resplendent color. John's vision of the "renewed city" is vibrant, an excess of reality as we know it. The jeweled foundation stones of the city beam radiant light through which

---

107. Revelation 13:5.

my imagination refracted a kaleidoscopic blaze of color. The sensual and extravagant nature of both the vision and the work suggest that our God makes not all new things, but all things new.

Scripture tells us of "the river of the water of life, bright as crystal, flowing from the throne of God and of the Lamb through the middle of the street of the city; also, on either side of the river, the tree of life with its twelve kinds of fruit, yielding its fruit each month; and the leaves of the tree were for the healing of the nations."[108]

The scriptural imagery of abundant fruit and medicinal leaves images the restoration of paradise heralded in The Epilogue. God's world, redeemed through the sacrificial lamb, is restored. It becomes the extravagant world of the eternal.

DVD Chapter 3: Paraments and Vestments

The last entry is a cope, commissioned by an Episcopal priest.[109] I wrote him the following letter:

> Dear Stuart,
> The church is replete with examples of art created solely for the purpose of glorifying God. Such examples range from those which contain recognizable ecclesial symbolism to those which reject it in favor of stating anew the enduring ideas encapsulated in scripture.
>
> This work of wearable art, tailored after the ecclesiastical cope, was inspired by the following doxology you selected from Ephesians 3:20-21, "Now to him who by the power at work within us is able to do far more abundantly than all we ask or think, to him be

---

108. Revelation 22:1–2.
109. Cope: a long cape worn over vestments as outerwear.

glory in the church and in Christ Jesus to all generations, for ever and ever." This cope, inspired by this scripture, is a statement about life transformed by God.

God is symbolized by all that is gold, by that material which is most radiant. It winds its way through the cope, symbolic of God's presence.

The changing shapes of flat colors represent the different challenges of life while the strands of color represent the individual. In all instances, these strands of color, either knotted or flowing, are different in color from the color to which they adhere. This difference symbolizes the change, the transformation of life empowered by the Spirit of God. On the orphrey banding where the knots of gold represent God's companioning in the challenges of life, the strands of color not only change but also move in sequence from dark to light. Everywhere all colors form a pattern of movement from dark to light as testimony to a life seeking enlightenment. The same symbolic scheme occurs in the hood. The morse, the gold clasp which functions to secure the cope in place, signs a life held together by trust in the Word.

DVD Chapter 4: Temporary Installations

The works in chapter 4 all share in common a limited life. Actually, this statement is only partially true. Unknown to me until after the fact, the three sides of the altar frontal for the Walter Reed Army Medical Center's Easter morning sunrise service were enclosed in Plexiglas. It is the last work pictured in this chapter. After its encasement, it was hung over the entrance to the hospital in its large atrium lobby. It hangs there today.

The *Last Supper*, the sixth work pictured in this chapter, was commissioned by the leadership of Presbyterian Women. Initially owned by them, they rented it several times to other churches and church conferences. Then they returned it to my studio for storage, where it remains.

The ninth work in this chapter was conceived and fabricated at Holden Village, a Lutheran retreat center in the middle of Washington State. I lived there as a short-term member of its faculty in one of its small chalets nestled against the mountainside. Next door to me lived the resident musician. Nearby was the retreat center's clothes closet where a hodgepodge of discarded items existed. One day I cleared out the minimalist furnishings in my living room. I retrieved jeans, socks, scarves, etc. from the clothes closet, cut them up, and configured them on the floor to create the banner that is pictured. I could not find, however, the dark blue material I thought best for the arms of this work (in actuality a self-portrait) among the discarded stuff. In the midst of my frustration, the musician walked in, peered at the floor, and said, "Don't worry. We are a sacrificial community." He ran next door, retrieved a very fine blue shirt, and handed it over.

Such encounters make the doing of this work worth it.

Chapter 5: Banners

The second banner shown in the section of individual banners interprets Philippians 2:5–11, known as the Christ Hymn. Required to do an exegetical study of a passage of scripture when a seminary student, I chose this Philippians passage.[110] I also remember thinking what an interesting visual challenge it would be to exegete this passage in a non-verbal vocabulary. So I did. I hung the banner outside the classroom for a momentary class showing and handed over the following statement to my professor.

> "Have this mind among yourselves, which is yours in Christ Jesus, who, though he was in the form of God, did not count equality with God a thing to be grasped, but emptied himself, taking the form of a servant, being born in the likeness of men. And being found in human form he humbled himself and became

110. Exegete: one who practices exegesis, an explanation or critical interpretation of a text.

obedient unto death, even death on a cross. Therefore God has highly exalted him and bestowed on him the name which is above every name, that at the name of Jesus every knee should bow, in heaven and on earth and under the earth, and every tongue confess that Jesus Christ is Lord, to the glory of God the Father." (Philippians 2:5–11)

The consensus of modern scholarship states that Philippians 2:5–11 is a pre-Pauline Christological hymn. The language inherent in this hymn is that of humiliation and exaltation, not crucifixion and resurrection. This hymn sings of the Christ event as the definitive saving event through which the Kingdom of God enters into the earthly realm and triumphs victoriously over the powers of darkness.

The reasons for illustrating the Philippian hymn this way are as follows: from the start, I decided to use a full color palette (multiple hues) along with a full range of intensities and values. How could a cosmic picture be otherwise? Furthermore, because of its cosmic dimension, it seemed appropriate to scale down in size the body of Christ and to focus on the visual union of humiliation with exaltation. Since the essence of the hymn is movement between the realms of heaven and earth, a dominant descending movement resulting in an exploding ascending movement became the artistic device used to proclaim the humiliation/exaltation theme.

"In the form of God" presupposes the pre-existence of Christ and consequently testifies to a highly developed Christology. The issue belongs to being and the essence of that being finds its symbol at the top of the tapestry headlining the dominant descending thrust of movement. This area is white. It is white because white exists in that material which reflects, which emits the whole spectrum of energy waves we perceive as color when such waves are isolated one from another. Color is a quality of light and does not exist apart from light. White therefore holds no color rays unto itself but symbolically speaking gives color to the world in the form of light. This descent begun in the heavens sinks into the earthly realm and ultimately into the all-consuming blackness via that material which absorbs, which swallows up all the energy waves of light. Absence of color symbolically means absence of light. Thus Christ descends from high glory (light/God) to the nadir of abasement (darkness/death). His cross exists in the earthly sphere, in the lower half of the picture plane.

This hymn sings of Christ's radical act of obedience. Consequently, the work emphasizes the Christ figure undergoing death. Enveloped in cool dark colors, his symbolic figural presence sinks into the bowels of the earth.

But the hymn does not end here. The cross is perceived as a God event. Light explodes around and through the cross, and in the explosion of this light aided by warm colors of the spectrum, red, orange, and yellow, the new reality breaks in, interpenetrating and ultimately moving beyond the colors of darkness. The greater visual strength of the warm and light colors symbolically overpowers the dark colors. Since a light color emanates from the painted poles holding up the banner at the top, explicit in the piece is the sense that every tongue will confess that Jesus Christ is Lord. He is the light of the world; it is this light which I have tried to capture in the work through the paradox of the cross.

The eighth entry under the individual banner section is a design model created in sections for a weekly chapel service in an Episcopal day school. Children were asked to respond visually to the hymn text "All Things Bright and Beautiful." Images were harvested from their contributions and were transcribed exactly as given. In this instance of participatory aesthetics, the mothers of the children fabricated the work. Each section (banner) of the work matches exactly the in-scale color model.

DVD Chapter 6: Creative Process

The first work shown is a design for a work of participatory aesthetics, now nearly completed by the community as a needlepointed tapestry. It was conceived in a circular format with an intended 11' diameter. The finished work will fill the back wall of a large urban church's chapel, opposing its large entrance doors of glass. Not far from these doors and directly opposing them are another set of large glass doors. They open onto a busy downtown street in Greensboro, NC. The community wanted a visible work of welcoming.

My creative process undergirding this work commenced with the creation of a grid, a division of our agreed-upon circular format, into discreet sections for the purpose of accommodating many stitchers. A dozen drawings ensued and all were jettisoned because the repetition of rectangles and squares, no matter how creatively organized, did not provide a dynamic structure into which I could image a work of welcome. Eventually, the evolution of curving elements to the grid was not only liberating but also suggested that a substructure of parallel vertical and horizontal lines in the tapestry would provide cohesiveness between the grid and tapestry images. The grid design utilized yields 45 separate sections, yielding ample opportunity for community participation.[111]

Next, I read scripture and drew my responses, all the while struggling to discern what these stories suggested for visualiza-

---

111. The grid is made of wood, as is the circular border. Although they appear as white in the in-scale paper model shown, they are lacquered in a color not yet selected at the time this model was presented. The grid's 45 sections offer 45 people the opportunity to needlepoint.

tion and what at the same time would fit into the grid structure. I decided to experiment with images and symbols inspired by: the creation story in Genesis; the relationship of crucifixion/resurrection; the sacraments of baptism and communion; and the intentionality of God as manifested through Holy Scripture and the Holy Spirit. As my drawings were refined and more thought about the interconnectedness of images ensued, I decided to draw all symbolic representations of the story within squares (the edges of which when combined with other squares would constitute the vertical and horizontal substructure being sought). Once all the elements of the story were drawn, a Xerox machine reproduced each drawing in about ten different sizes.

At this point in the process, I decided to work in 1/3 scale. Enlarging my grid drawing to a 44" diameter, I experimented with the placement of differently sized empty squares on it. Meanwhile I also created an in-scale value study comprised of fifteen different shades of gray paper ranging from very dark to very light plus black and white paper. This exercise provided a guidepost for later organization of color.

I returned to the 44" diameter grid drawing and began the slow and complex process of filling in each section with imagery based on my prior drawings and experimentations with scale. Weeks later when this part of the process was complete, I translated all the images a section at a time into color. After a while, I had to work on multiple sections simultaneously in order to control the passage of colors from one group to another and at the same time revise my drawings continuously to accommodate new insights accrued along the way.

My love-hate relationship with rubber cement continued. The fragility of the finished design required a solution for shipment and handling. I adhered the design to a ½" piece of foam-core board and pinned it into place with scores of ½" straight pins rather than glue. By this point in time, I could bear neither the smell nor the touch of rubber cement! With the in-scale color model, I included the following statement of explication:

> This design is conceived to speak from different distances. From a far distance, the viewer will wonder what the vibrant shimmering work

is all about. At an intermediate distance, symbol and sign will begin to disclose themselves, and the numerous visual transparencies will evoke a sense of veiled mystery. At close range, "the darkness on the face of the deep" gives way to an inbreaking of light. Dry land appears, as does all of creation in its myriad of complexity. God (designated in Hebrew at the left) pronounces that creation is good. In two small sections of the grid, the temptation and fall are glimpsed through Adam, Eve, and the apple.

Other sections are self-evident if one is initiated into the story. The theme of Pentecost, a symbol for the creation of the church, hovers above the scene of Calvary. Let your imagination have free reign as you meander through all the sections.

"It can be laid down as a pretty reliable rule that while artists usually mean what they say, they do not always say exactly what they mean. They may be playing with us only to keep our interest or leading us down enticing bypaths for the sake of a later rendezvous. An authentic work of art has both a surface and a depth, and the relation between them may not be a matter of direct progression at all, but a broken line of indirect suggestion."[112]

The fourth work shown in this chapter is the very first work I documented, urged to do so as has been said by a faculty colleague. This work is a 22' x 60' stage backdrop for a Triennial Conference of Presbyterian Women. Students saw how the conference theme ("I am bread in the hands of God for the world") played out. Initially paralyzed by the thought of undertaking such a large work, I sought rational sense in the library of what the Eucharist means despite the fact that I had participated in it all of my life. Eventually I

112. Roger Hazelton, *A Theological Approach to Art* (Nashville: Abingdon Press, 1967), p. 27.

discerned the notion that the Eucharist is a way of remembering the past, living in the present, and empowering the future. Thinking of the past, I immediately thought of Da Vinci's *Last Supper*, an image that has passed into popular consciousness and that has been copied many times after Da Vinci's original. (In fact, Andy Warhol spent the last years of his life working with this image.) Moreover, it provided a horizontal axis of design, which was precisely what was needed to fill the stage of Purdue University's Music Hall, where the conference took place. At this point in the process, I had a handle on how to move towards a finished work. The DVD shows how I began, where I went, and what happened. What it does not show is that the materials used were flame retardant, a severely limiting condition of the commission. This chapter also shows other creative processes and ends with a few samples of design boards, the kind an artist might submit to a church committee.

DVD Chapter 7: Designs of Works in Progress

The second work shown is a developing installation of participatory aesthetics.

> This installation, changeable with each liturgical season, relies on non-objective imagery to provide a meaning-making opportunity for the congregation. It speaks through the power of suggestion emanating from visual repetitions of the circle, an archetypal symbol for completeness and union with God. Each season is imaged using expressive configurations of parts of circular lines and edges juxtaposed and/or intersecting.
>
> The panels, in their seasonal aggregates, speak of the mysterious activity of God. The work builds to a climax in the last liturgical season wherein the Trinity emerges as three complete interlocking circles. The blue of the creator God of Advent, the gold of the Redeemer God of Lent, and the red of the

Spirit/Sustainer God of Pentecost adhere in one another.

The cycle begins with Advent, a time of expectant waiting for the in-breaking of the Kingdom of God. These panels, with their highlights of gold, hint at the anticipated coming of the Messiah, while visually ushering in the activity of God.

At Christmas, heaven and earth meet in the birth of the Christ child. The intersecting circles anticipate the place of the Messiah in Trinitarian formulation, just as the perpendicular lines of the square eschatalogically point toward Calvary. Simultaneously, the circle within the square focuses on the radical otherness of the miracle of this child.

In Lent, intersecting edges of circles shape suggestive motifs of the palms thrown by the multitudes who welcomed Christ into Jerusalem. Good Friday finds expression in the perpendicular intersections of deep purple colors.

Easter is configured of particular panels from each of the other seasons plus two new bracketing panels at either end of the installation. The agitated lines sitting in front of the complete circle on one end panel mimic the activity at the tomb while the other end panel suggests an empty tomb. The theological intent of presenting an Easter image comprised of visual parts shows that the events of each liturgical season conspire in the triumph of Easter. Pentecost is an unbridled, ecstatic portrayal of the Spirit of God at work cascading into our lives, combusting, and unleashing life giving energy.

The panels of the Season After Pentecost further articulate the powerful and almighty activity of God while simultaneously suggest centuries of Christian history and tradition which have mitigated our understanding of who God is.

EPILOGUE:

Sending Forth

But yield who will to their separation,
My object in living is to unite
My avocation and my vocation
As my two eyes make one in sight.
Only where love and need are one,
And the work is play for mortal stakes,
Is the deed ever really done
For heaven and the future's sakes.[113]

This book of musings and memoir is a benediction on lived experience; like all creative efforts, it evolved out of the expenditure of living. The looking back necessitated by this effort enlivens future imaginings. My studio, with its neglected 24" bed etching press and 60" vertical tapestry loom, postures possibilities as binding as Kathy's bidding. I cannot nor could not loosen the grip of either enjoining.

Neither can I relinquish my hope that the church will seek relationships with contemporary artists, that the art world will look favorably upon the confessing artist, and that theological education will eschew its condescension towards practice.

Meanwhile, I still hope to create a funeral pall. Loving into existence a work of materials transformed teaches one about the art of living. Threaded in and out of the fabric of both is the God who in the beginning made all things and in the end says, "Behold, I make all things new."[114]

---

113. Robert Frost *Selected Poems of Robert Frost*, with introduction by Robert
    Graves (New York: Holt, Rinehart and Winston, 1963), p. 180.
114. Revelation 21:5.

Outline of *DVD* Chapters

*B*elow is an outline of the DVD chapters and the churches, organizations, or institutions that commissioned the artwork.

Chapter 1: Transforming Liturgical Space

1. Peace Lutheran Church, Alexandria, VA

2. Metropolitan Memorial United Methodist Church, Washington, DC

3. Kennedy Heights Presbyterian Church, Cincinnati, OH

4. Braddock Street United Methodist Church, Winchester, VA

5. Abiding Presence Lutheran Church, Beltsville, MD

6. Immaculate Conception Roman Catholic Church, Towson, MD

7. Gladwynne Presbyterian Church, Gladwynne, PA

8. First Presbyterian Church, Winchester, VA

9. Governor's Island Coast Guard Chapel, Governor's Island, NY

10. St. John's Episcopal Church, Avon, CT

11. Asbury Village United Methodist Retirement Home, Gaithersburg, MD

12. Arlington Unitarian Universalist Church, Arlington, VA

13. B'nai Israel Synagogue, Rockville, MD

Chapter 2: Transforming Other Ecclesial Space

Narthex

1. Grace Episcopal Church, Baldwinsville, NY

2. Shallowford Presbyterian Church, Shallowford, NC

3. Good Shepherd Roman Catholic Church, Mt. Vernon, VA

Balcony

4. Bethesda United Methodist Church, Bethesda, MD

Sanctuary Entrance

5. Christ the Redeemer Roman Catholic Church, Sterling, VA

6. Bethesda Presbyterian Church, Bethesda, MD

Chapel

7. Yale Divinity School's Marquand Chapel, New Haven, CT

8. Centreville United Methodist Church, Centreville, VA

Church Hallways

9. Westmarket Street United Methodist Church Day Care Center, Greensboro, NC

Fellowship Hall

10. Falls Church Presbyterian Church, Falls Church, VA

Chapter 3: Paraments and Vestments

Paraments

1. Garrett Evangelical Seminary, Evanston, IL

2. Asbury Village United Methodist Retirement Home, Gaithersburg, MD

3. Calvary United Methodist Church, Annapolis, MD

4. Avon Episcopal Church, Avon, CT

5. Second Presbyterian Church, Baltimore, MD

6. Westmoreland Congregational Church, Chevy Chase, MD

Paraments and Vestments

7. Rayne Memorial United Methodist Church, New Orleans, LA

8. Episcopal Church of the Nativity, Camp Springs, MD

9. Gettysburg Lutheran Seminary, Gettysburg, PA

Vestments

10. Stoles

11. Chasuble

12. Cope

Chapter 4: Temporary Installations

Convention Centers

1. Presbyterian Women's Conference, Commonwealth Convention Center, Louisville, KY

2. The United Methodist National Student Conference, A. J. Cervantes Convention and Exhibition Center and the Sheraton Hotel Lobby, St. Louis, MO

3. United Methodist Church's celebration of the 1989 Hymnal, Constitution Hall, Washington, DC

4. The United Methodist Global Gathering, Civic Center, Indianapolis, IN

5. Presbyterian Youth Conference, Purdue University Music Hall, West Lafayette, IN

6. Presbyterian Women's Conference, Purdue University Music Hall, West Lafayette, IN

Retreat Centers

7. Lake Junaluska United Methodist Retreat Center, Lake Junaluska, NC

8. Montreat Presbyterian Retreat Center, Montreat, NC

9. Holden Village Lutheran Retreat Center, Chelan, WA

Outdoor Sites

10. Walter Reed Army Medical Center, Washington, DC

Chapter 5: Banners

1. John Wesley Bicentennial Celebration Banner, Dallas, TX (now residing at The United Methodist Archives, Drew University, Madison, NJ)

2. National Naval Medical Center Chapel, Bethesda, MD

3. Marvin Memorial United Methodist Church, Silver Spring, MD

4. Episcopal Bicentennial Convention Banners, Baltimore, MD

5. Banners

  a. COSROW, The Commission on the Status and Role of Women, Baltimore, MD

  b. Christ Hymn, privately owned

  c. Crucified Christ, Homewood—at Williamsport Chapel, Williamsport, PA

  d. Trinity Lutheran Easter Banner, Rockville, MD

  e. St. Elizabeth Roman Catholic Church Easter Banner, Rockville, MD

  f. St. Matthias Roman Catholic Church Easter Banner, Lanham, MD

  g. Church Street United Methodist Church Music Banner, Knoxville, TN

  h. Grace Episcopal Day School Banner, Kensington, MD

  i. St. John's Episcopal Church, Norwood, Chevy Chase, MD

  j. Grace Church/Christ Church, Kilmarnack Episcopal Church Complex, Kilmarnack, VA

  k. College of Preachers, Washington National Cathedral, Washington, DC

Chapter 6: Creative Process

1. Westmarket Street United Methodist Church, Greensboro, NC

2. Grace Episcopal Church, Baldwinsville, NY

3. Christ Hymn—privately owned

4. Presbyterian Women's Conference, Purdue University Music Hall, West Lafayette, IN

5. Abiding Presence Lutheran Church, Beltsville, MD

6. Peace Lutheran Church, Alexandria, VA (Design Boards)

Chapter 7: Designs of Works in Progress

1. Kennedy Heights Presbyterian Church, Cincinnati, OH

2. Westminster Presbyterian Church, Greensboro, NC

3. Good Shepherd Episcopal Church, Silver Spring, MD

4. Westmarket Street United Methodist Church, Greensboro, NC

5. Garrett Evangelical Seminary Hallway, Evanston, IL

DATE DUE

GAYLORD — PRINTEL